# A Question of Class

# A Question of Class:
## The Redneck Stereotype in Southern Fiction

Duane Carr

Bowling Green State University Popular Press
Bowling Green, OH 43403

Chapter 9 appears in a slightly different form in the Spring 1996 issue of *Mississippi Quarterly*, and chapter 16 will appear as an article in a forthcoming issue of *Midwest Quarterly*.

Copyright © 1996 Bowling Green State University Popular Press

Library of Congress Cataloging-in-Publication Data
Carr, Duane.
    A question of class : the Redneck stereotype in southern fiction / Duane Carr.
        p.        cm.
    Includes bibliographical references and index.
    ISBN 0-87972-721-7. -- ISBN 0-87972-722-5 (pbk.)
    1. American fiction--Southern States--History and criticism.
2. Literature and society--Southern States. 3. Stereotype (Psychology) in literature. 4. Working class whites in literature. 5. Southern States --In literature. 6. Social classes in literature. 7. Rednecks--Southern States. 8. Poor in literature. I. Title.
PS261.C37  1996
813.009'353--dc20                                          96-38510
                                                                CIP

Cover design by Gary Dumm/Dumm Art

# Contents

## Part Three: Reinforcing the Stereotype

## Part Four: Overcoming the Stereotype

# Preface

It might seem at first glance that I have used "redneck" and "poor white" interchangeably in this work. There is a reason for this. "Poor white" is the term most writers and critics have used in the past to describe disadvantaged and dispossessed southern white citizens. The problem is that the term now appears somewhat old-fashioned and, despite the original intent, has evolved into a largely derogatory term. "Redneck," on the other hand, has come into use more recently by some historians and social critics to describe not only the earlier "poor whites" but what might be seen as their descendants, working-class whites who may have decent jobs, especially when compared to an older generation, but who have maintained an identity with the original group. One reason for this identification is that the psychological wounds of the "poor white" experience are often passed from generation to generation.

I admit, however, a reluctance to use either term. At the same time, the more neutral terms "disadvantaged" and/or "dispossessed" have proven awkward in most instances. It has therefore seemed appropriate and more natural to use "poor white" when discussing authors and historians of the eighteenth, nineteenth, and early twentieth centuries, acknowledging in this way their use of the term, and to reserve "redneck" for the sections on more recent literature. As will be noted, I have, in each instance, felt a need to enclose both terms in quotation marks.

The book is divided into four parts, each representing a specific period in southern literary history—the antebellum, post-Civil War, modern, and contemporary. The chapters that introduce the various periods lay the historical and sociological groundwork for the discussions of individual writers that follow.

I have treated the authors in chronological order, except for Warren and Arnow, whom I have placed in the last section as forerunners of the contemporary attitude.

I am indebted to David Lee and Carlton Jackson of the history department of Western Kentucky University for encouragement and helpful suggestions, also to Sue Bridwell Beckham of the English department at the University of Wisconsin-Stout for a careful reading of the manuscript and an invaluable critique.

# Part One:

# Establishing the Stereotype

# 1

# The Nature of the Stereotype

The poorest of working-class whites of both town and country have long been degraded in southern literature. Tapped "sand hillers," "tackies," "hillbillies," "wool hats," "tar heels," "clay eaters," "dirt eaters," "peckerwoods," "lintheads," and more recently, "trailer park trash" and "rednecks," they have been most often depicted, from William Byrd in the eighteenth century to Cormac McCarthy in our own, as simple-minded, shiftless, lazy and violent—a subspecies to be detested and ridiculed or, on rare occasions, felt sorry for.

Making the poor the butt of jokes is not unique to the American South, of course. Juvenal noted the trend in first-century Rome and castigated his fellow citizens for their thoughtless jibes at the unfortunate. "Cheerless poverty has no harder trial," he wrote in *Satires III*, than in its making "men the subject of ridicule."

Sociologists Michael Morris and John B. Williamson have traced the particular disdain that Americans have toward the poor to the influence of Luther and Calvin in sixteenth- and seventeenth-century Europe when traditional Catholic views emphasizing charity were challenged by the Protestant ethic, which taught that God rewards hard work and that "the greater the material rewards received, the greater the extent to which the individual was doing God's will by being industrious." Poverty thus became a sign of God's disapproval. This view "provided an ideological buttress for repressive policies toward the 'undeserving poor'" (414).

It is not hard to see how this attitude became a part of America's thinking through the influence of the Puritans. "Seventeenth century colonial spokesmen," writes historian Neil Betten, "condemned the vast majority of the destitute as lazy and immoral." Betten adds that historians "have often pointed to this attitude among the Puritan elite of New England" (1).

3

It is also not hard to see how the notion was reinforced through the doctrines of the Social Darwinists of the late nineteenth century who believed that poor people were the weak elements of society to be left alone to die out, all for the good of humanity as a whole. G. Archibald Reid, for example, in a 1906 article in the *American Journal of Sociology*, argued against social programs to help the poor because "an improved environment tends ultimately to degrade the race by causing an increased survival of the unfit" (qtd. in Degler 43).

He was not alone in this sentiment. In fact, this was a major theme of American geneticists of the early part of this century who viewed intelligence and the capacity to get ahead as inherited traits, leading them to form a committee of the American Breeders' Association to "investigate and report on heredity in the human race" and to make clear "the value of superior blood and the menace of inferior blood" (Degler 41).

In literature, more often than not, the southern "poor whites" are seen, not only as inferior but as almost another breed. James Dickey reflects such an attitude in an interview in which he defended his characterizations of the "hillbillies" who senselessly and without provocation attack the middle-class protagonists of *Deliverance:*

You know, there's some kind of absolutism about country people. . . . there's almost no hill family, or 'crackers' as we call them at home, that doesn't have at least one relative in prison. . . . Life and death up in those Georgia hill counties, life and death are very basic gut-type things, and if somebody does something that violates your code, you kill him, and you don't think twice about it. (Heyen 153)

This comment, which Dickey rendered as an observation, is really only one more repetition of a much over-worked stereotype of hill people as "outlanders" whose behavior seems foreign to urban dwellers. And since few urban dwellers ever strike up an acquaintance with an "outlander," "observations" made from whatever distance are, more often than not, derived from preconceived notions based on past experience, not with life in the hills, but with literature, the movies, and television. Sadly, Dickey's interviewer assured him that his characterizations of the "two hillbillies" were "wonderfully realized."

Interestingly enough, another southerner who has lived and taught school for many years among those very north Georgia "hillbillies" that Dickey depicts, sees them in a totally different light. "Mountain people," he writes, "have a healthy tolerance for those whose lifestyle differs from theirs. It is one of their most commendable traits." They are, in fact, "far more tolerant than the national stereotype would have the outside world believe" (Wiggonton 163-65).

Nor are the rural poor the only ones subject to stereotyping, for people categorized as "rednecks" and "trailer park trash" often live on the outskirts of towns and cities and sometimes earn livings that place them in the lower-middle or working class. Nonetheless, because they are ill-educated and speak nonstandard English, more prosperous citizens often tend to see them as simply offspring of the earlier "hillbillies."

In addition, urbanites frequently view all people from southern rural areas and small towns as generally inferior types and the subject more of jokes than of serious consideration. Bobbie Ann Mason gives a vivid illustration of this in the short story "State Champions," in which she depicts an encounter in upstate New York between her protagonist, who has attended high school in "a tiny community with a couple of general stores" and a fellow Kentuckian who has a seemingly more urban background. The man, engaging in an obvious stereotype, categorizes the state-champion basketball team of the protagonist's high-school as "a handful of country boys who could barely afford basketball shoes," then proceeds to tell a joke in which one of the boys is able to make "a two-hand set shot from midcourt" simply because it is the first time he has tried it indoors with no wind blowing. One detects in the account Mason's barely suppressed anger at such smug ignorance.

Unfortunately, many authors do not write about rural people from first-hand experience. Instead they too often assume they already "know" these people in the same way so many whites of all classes assumed—before the civil rights movement of the sixties, at least—that they "knew" African-Americans. Flannery O'Connor satirizes such an attitude in "Good Country People" when she has the naive but well-meaning Mrs. Hopewell exclaim that she has had "plenty of experience with trash" and needs no further education on the way their minds work, finding it easier to fall back on culturally ingrained stereotypes than to treat her workers as individuals. Even her use of the term "good country people" to designate farmers she feels are a cut above "trash" is, in itself, condescending.

All too often, fiction writers fall back on Mrs. Hopewell's train of thought. They aren't alone, of course, for the sad fact is that stereotyped depictions have appeared not only in novels and short stories but in all varieties of the media from movies to comic strips. As I.A. Newby points out, "even sympathetic historians still grant something to that negative image" ("Getting at the History of Poor Whites" 81).

This has been the case for some time, of course. John Crowe Ransom, in *I'll Take My Stand* (1930), spoke of the poorest whites as a different "strain" from the "better classes." They emerged, he speculated, from the "apparently stagnant sections of mankind," which also include "the heathen Chinee" and "the Roman Catholic Mexican" (Twelve Southerners 23, 10). John Gould Fletcher, in the same volume, wondered why we bother to send rural children to school at all since they are, in his view, uneducable. The purpose of education, he wrote, is "to bring out something that is already potentially existent in the human being." In the case of rural children, there is "nothing to begin with," hence "no amount of education can do . . . any good." These children are part of a class Fletcher dubbed "inferior," and "the inferior," he maintained, "should exist only for the sake of the superior." He postulated that instead of trying to educate farm children, we should leave them to their "ploughing and washing dishes" (93, 119).

Writing a few years after Ransom and Fletcher, Shields McIlwain, in his often sympathetic treatment of the "poor whites" of southern literature, nonetheless freely used such terms as "trash," "bumpkins," "laggards," "slovenly outlanders," "sorry southerners," and "tackies" without reservation, as if they were unbiased and perfectly acceptable to his readers. He, in fact, condemned Joel Chandler Harris's sympathetic portrayals of hill people as examples of a naive author growing "misty-eyed over Cracker halfwits." He went on to praise Erskine Caldwell and William Faulkner for not succumbing to such sentimentality and for realizing how "stupid" and "slow-witted" the "poor whites" actually are, a realization he felt was missing in the works of Ellen Glasgow, among others (219).

As late as 1980, J.V. Ridgely acclaimed William Byrd's eighteenth-century stereotyped depictions of North Carolina "lubbers" as highly accurate, concluding that "we are fortunate that such a clear-eyed man as Byrd was on hand to set it down" (11-12). And he is not alone. In fact, the widespread agreement with Byrd's depictions accounts for much in southern fiction that has been characterized as "grotesque," a characterization C. Hugh Holman, incidentally, sees as erroneous. He quotes Flannery O'Connor to the effect that "any fiction that comes out of the South is going to be called grotesque by northern readers," and he defends Thomas Wolfe against the charge of stereotyping his mountain characters by asserting that those characterizations are accurate pictures of "tormented, twisted, and diseased lives which most of us can recognize as actually existing and within our experience" (30-31).

F.N. Boney, who brings "first-hand, on-the scene testimony" to his defense of "rednecks," explains stereotyping by otherwise literate academicians as a manifestation of the need felt by "every good American" to look down on a "mudsill." "Most American opinion-makers who specialize in moral judgments," he writes, "agree that the infamous redneck belongs high on any list of leading despicable types" (4, 31).

Will D. Campbell, who lays claim to a "redneck heritage," is justifiably angry with academics as well as other professionals, and he adds his voice to Boney's in asking why the "redneck" stereotype has persisted among the educated while other stereotypes, such as those of African-Americans and Jews, have been slowly disappearing. "Like the nouns *nigger* and *kike*," he writes, "*redneck* is most often used pejoratively." He continues:

As a descendant of people disparaged by that word, I ask why the first two terms are eschewed by even the most blatantly racist and bigoted publications, while *redneck* is used routinely in virtually every respectable, sophisticated, and allegedly responsible newspaper and magazine in America. (92)

Jeremy Iggers puts it well. "Hatred of the poor," he says, may well be the "last acceptable bigotry" (145).

In order to come to grips with this particular stereotype, however, we need to examine the nature of stereotypes in general. These persist, according to Walter Lippmann, because in a world of "buzzing confusion, the attempt to see all things freshly and in detail, rather than in types and generalities, is exhausting." For this reason we are all, to some extent at least, "hurried observers," accepting for the sake of convenience stereotypes "already defined" for us by culture. "We do not first see, then define, "he maintains, "we define first and then see" (89, 81).

The function of a stereotype, according to psychologist Gordon W. Allport, is to justify or rationalize our acceptance or rejection of a particular group. It also acts as "a screening or selective device to maintain simplicity in perception and in thinking." Moreover, stereotypes serve "as projective screens for our personal conflict" and they continue to exist because "they are socially supported, continually revived and hammered in . . . by novels, short stories, newspaper items, movies, stage, radio, and television" (191, 200). Allen W. Batteau writes, regarding stereotypes of the poor in Appalachia: "For different groups in our society, various texts provide an archetypal reality." This "reality," once created, "assumes an autonomous character." Observers, writers among them, see what they expect to see (13).

But why, to restate Campbell's question, has the stereotype of the "redneck" persisted while other degrading stereotypes have, to a great extent, disappeared, at least overtly, among educated people?

One reason may be that the civil rights movement, which jolted so many whites into sensitivity toward African-Americans, rarely addressed issues surrounding disadvantaged whites. Another explanation may lie in Campbell's contention that "rednecks . . . have become convenient scapegoats for the subtle institutionalized racism that has replaced Jim Crow. In common usage, redneck has become synonymous with racist and bigot" (93).

Another reason may be the desire on the part of a great many southerners to hold on to a caste system that is part of the South's heritage. Indeed, those who look back upon the Old South as being close to an ideal society have witnessed the collapse of the structure upon which that society was based. It has, in fact, been slowly eroding almost from the beginning, first with the extension of voting rights to the "common man," then with the freeing of the slaves, and finally with integration. Each of these steps toward democracy was a blow to those who wished to maintain something of the old caste system, which had clearly drawn the line between the "superior" and the "inferior" classes. If we finally remove the line that divides the "respectable" people from the "trash," then what is left of the old system in which, to paraphrase Ransom, each class was content to remain in its respective "place?"

But as a number of recent historians have pointed out, the Old South was not the idyllic society apologists have wanted us to believe existed. For one thing, as William R. Taylor notes, "The men who originated [the Cavalier ideal] were not aristocratic in any sense which Europeans would have recognized" (319). And who can now believe that slaves were content to stay in their "place"? Fewer realize, of course, that disadvantaged whites were not content either. Witness, for example, Andrew Lytle's assertion in *I'll Take My Stand* that before the war they had happily accepted their "inferiority" to the planter and had lost their contentment only when they moved down from the hills to farm the sectioned land of the old plantations, acquiring in the process a corruptive concern for making money—a concern Lytle believed neither the "poor whites" nor the "aristocrats" had in those idyllic days of the Old South (213-15).

The fact is there was a great deal of discontent among dispossessed whites of the antebellum South. Fanny Kemble, the British actress, for one, wrote in her 1839 journal of having observed a number of "pinelanders" in Georgia who were "wretched, degraded," and "miserable." Too poor to possess land or slaves, and having no means of living in the towns, they had to squat on the land of others, erecting "crude structures" and wearing "tatters" (110-11, 182).

And historian Fred Arthur Bailey, in *Class and Tennessee's Confederate Generation*, analyzes a questionnaire given to Confederate veterans who were asked to recall their prewar experiences. No "contentment" appears in any of the landless whites' memories of those antebellum days. Instead what Bailey found were "strong negative attitudes" on the part of a "significant portion of the poor and a few from the other social classes" toward the "tremendous gulf [that] separated the poor, who inhabited meager log hovels, and the rich, who resided in magnificent frame mansions." Moreover, these veterans "cast doubt on the fabled planter paternalism" and the status of the "yeoman," the small landowner celebrated by Daniel R. Hundley in the nineteenth century and by Frank Owsley in our own. Bailey, in fact, refutes Owsley's contention that these small landowners were part of a broad, relatively prosperous middle class who lived contented lives in harmony with the wealthy planters. "Yeomen" in reality, writes Bailey, were seldom more than subsistence farmers struggling to maintain "mere survival from generation to generation" (72-73, 21).[1]

Thus it is safe to say that the poorest whites, who, in the words of historian Francis Butler Simkins, were "genuine white southerners, as blond and sharp-featured as other Anglo-Saxons"

(139) could not have been much more "contented" with their lot before the war than after.

But something needs to be said to explain how a group of white farmers, otherwise indistinguishable from their wealthier plantation-owning cousins, descended into degrading poverty and a life style that made them into stereotypes in the eyes of others. Contemporary historians have explained this phenomenon through a series of events, beginning with the system of slavery and the one-crop methods of the antebellum South. J. Wayne Flynt explains:

On the Southern frontier, planters and farmers concentrated on maximizing profits. They invested little of their capital in maintaining soil productivity because it was cheaper to buy and improve new land than it was to take care of the old. Planters moving south and west to new plots left behind a trail of farmed-out soil that became the home of the poor whites. Virgin land in the hill regions quickly eroded and also reduced sturdy yeomen to impoverished subsistence farmers. (6)

Thus a method of farming that proved profitable to the earlier planters destroyed the latecomers and condemned them to poverty that increased with the years.

Moreover, farmers impoverished by depleted lands could not find employment elsewhere, for labor was done by slaves. Kenneth Stampp in *The Peculiar Institution* explains how farmers and planters not only utilized slavery for their own planting and harvesting but loaned out their field hands to nonslaveholding neighbors for a fee, or sometimes as a favor. People in town who wanted domestic servants hired them off the plantations, and the railroad owners who needed laborers recruited slaves "by promising their owners generous compensation" (70-71).

Clearly in such a system, there was no place for the laborer who wished to hire out for wages. Thus, for the failed farmer, unable to eke out a living on depleted soil, there was no place to go and nothing to do except to become a squatter on someone else's land. In addition, the Homestead Act, which should have rescued these poor farmers by giving them a piece of land in the West, was opposed by southern conservatives in Congress and the act failed to pass until after the South had seceded. Thus were the impoverished whites truly dispossessed.

The war only worsened their situation. As historian Jacqueline Jones has noted, many farmers, including the poor, returned from the war in 1865 too late to plant crops, which, of course, guaranteed their further plunge into poverty and dependence on the big landowners (65). Further, the end of slavery forced former plantation owners into debt, and those few who remained in farming overproduced cotton which, in turn, caused prices to plummet. At the same time, they replaced the slavery system by dividing the vast plantations into tenant farms.

Forrest McDonald and Grady McWhiney have traced the descent of these impoverished whites into further poverty during and after the war. First, advancing Union troops and retreating Confederates destroyed their livestock. Second, fencing laws, favored by the planters and forced through Congress after the war, ended antebellum open-range policy that had allowed small farmers to support their hogs. When these same farmers were forced to put their hogs into pens and expose them to heat, the hogs, who by nature required forest shade and moisture, acquired diseases which not only destroyed them but which they also passed on to the farmers and their families. Moreover, once these families were reduced to farming on shares, they found that they owed all to the great landowners who, in turn, were financed by northern creditors. And since the landowners were also store owners, they discouraged tenants from planting gardens, thereby forcing them to buy from the stores (1115-17). In addition, according to Simkins, the merchants and landowners found it easy to cheat the illiterate tenant farmers and did so on a large scale (334). As if the cards were not sufficiently stacked against them, the impoverished whites had also to compete with the newly freed slaves, who were preferred by most landowners as less rebellious workers.

On top of all this misery, the aristocracy succeeded in excluding dispossessed whites from the political process for many years by establishing poll taxes and literacy tests. As Simkins notes, government in the South became "the domain of a small but powerful elite, which used its institutions to dominate the poor of both races who were divided by racial animosity" (38). The practice of race-baiting by politicians, pitting working-class whites against African-Americans in order to control both, has been well documented. The entire process from beginning to the present day is described by Flynt as one of "downward mobility" (6).

Under such a system, it was inevitable that the dispossessed whites would become the object of scorn to their more fortunate neighbors. As Stampp explains:

> In a society of unequals—of privileged and inferior castes of wealth and poverty—the need to find some group to feel superior to is given a desperate urgency. And in some parts of Virginia even the field-hands who felt the contempt of the domestics could lavish their own contempt upon the "coal pit niggers" who were hired to work in the mines. Everywhere, slaves of all ranks ridiculed the non-slave-holder, especially the poor whites, the dregs of a stratified society, whom they scornfully called "po' buckra" and "white trash." (338)

Subsequent history has not been kind to the dispossessed whites either. With its disastrous one-crop farming methods, the South stayed poor even as the rest of the nation prospered. The Great Depression of the 1930s, which was a setback for the entire country, was a complete disaster for the South, where large numbers of tenant families, two-thirds of whom were white, lived on the border of starvation (Flynt 66-67). At the same time, coal miners in Appalachia, as well as workers throughout the South, found their per capita incomes drastically reduced.

These conditions played havoc with the health of those at the bottom of the economic scale, producing hookworm and malaria in countless thousands and forcing them to eat clay to survive. It was, however, as Simkins explains, a matter of "nutritional deficiencies, rather than moral degradation" on the part of the poor (139).

To add to the misery, New Deal programs were often subverted by landowners. In order to receive subsidies for not planting cotton, they simply moved their tenants off the land and plowed the cotton under. And when the Roosevelt administration introduced bills into Congress to sell land to tenant farmers, those bills were blocked or weakened by amendments offered by conservatives. That those same institutions provided the local structure through which federal programs were filtered also effectively weakened the 1960s War on Poverty programs (Flynt 82-83).

One would have expected the vast increase in industry moving south in recent decades to have improved the lot of the poor, but such has not been the case. According to Edward Flattau, the director of the Institute for Southern Studies, "unrestricted free enterprise," superimposed on a region "still heavily influenced by the Old South's basic tenets" has effectively kept wages low, benefits few, and unions out. And as rural sociologist Thomas A. Lyson notes, "the so-called free-market, supply-side microeconomic policies . . . during the 1980s have generally exacerbated the economic woes of families and communities in the rural South," putting them "into direct competition with the Third World countries for footloose industries," a competition southern communities could not win (xiv).

If, as C. Vann Woodward says, southern history "includes large components of frustration, failure, and defeat" as well as a "long and quite un-American experience with poverty" (127-28), then it is clearly the poorest of the poor who have felt the effects of that frustration and poverty the most. Unfortunately, this same group has been most scorned, condemned, and stereotyped by the rest of society. Samuel Johnson noted in the eighteenth century that it is bad enough being poor without having some blockhead laugh at you. Equally relevant is historian Carlton Jackson's comment that "at least ninety percent of the world's problems— not just the South's—come from people who express opinions without any factual knowledge behind them. Surely," he concludes, "this is the basis for all racial prejudice around the world, as well as for ethnic hatred."

My underlying assumption is that, in spite of the fact that the stereotype of the dispossessed and disadvantaged southern white may be firmly entrenched in the southern psyche, or for that matter in the psyche of the entire nation, enlightened and fair-minded people do not engage in stereotyping. And while we can readily admit that many among the most popular fiction writers have created, and continue to create, stereotypes, we should reserve our highest praise for those who, to use Lippmann's standard, "see all things freshly and in detail," transcending local prejudice to create art not of regional bias but of universal truth.

# 2

# William Byrd:
# The Dispossessed as Outlander

One of the earliest negative stereotypes of the poorest white population of the South was recorded by the Virginia planter William Byrd in his *History of the Dividing Line,* published posthumously in 1841. The book was made possible by Byrd's appointment as one of the commissioners who surveyed the disputed boundary line between Virginia and North Carolina in 1728. His broadly grotesque caricatures of North Carolina "lubbers" contained in that volume have often been cited as proof that "poor whites" have always been "trashy." Carl Hollidy, for example, in *A History of Southern Literature* (1906), asserted that Byrd's "facts about men, customs, animals" and "a host of subjects" were recorded "accurately and tersely" (63).

But as Kenneth S. Lynn has demonstrated, Byrd's "observations" were actually creative embellishments of skeletal diary entries made during the expedition. The diary entries took satiric aim at his fellow commissioners. It was only when he expanded the text for publication—with an eye toward his British readership—that he softened the satire against his fellow Virginians and created broad, grotesquely "comic" caricatures of the backwoods frontiersmen of North Carolina, using as his model Petronius, author of the *Satyricon* (14-15).

Unfortunately, by attempting to imitate such a model, and further, by seeking to impress a "sophisticated" London audience—who were accustomed to broad and often savage satire such as that of William Wycherly, and who relished negative portraits of Americans in general—Byrd succeeded in creating crude stereotypes of lazy mountaineers that have become prototypes for a seemingly endless parade of writers and cartoonists. They, like Byrd, have created their fictional "types" in the privacy of their studies, and they, like Byrd, have often been praised for the "truth" of their "observations."

Oddly enough, Byrd's contention that "'tis a thorough Aversion to Labor that makes People file off to N Carolina, where Plenty and a warm sun confirm them in their Disposition to Laziness for their whole Lives" contradicts another statement he makes in the same volume about "wretchedly poor" subsistence farmers trying to make a living on sandy soil that could "not bring potatoes." Such land would not seem to have offered "Plenty" in any sense of the word, given Byrd's own assertion that even "the best Estate affords little more than a coarse subsistence." Furthermore, people who gather "Knots of Light wood in Abundance, which they burn into tar and then carry to Norfolk or Nansimond for a Market" do not appear to be lazy (90-92).

In a further "observation" he set a standard of portraiture easily recognizable in a vast array of fiction, comic strips, movies, and television:

The men, for their Parts, just like the Indians impose all the Work upon the poor Women. They make their Wives rise out of their Beds early in the Morning, at the same time that they lye and Snore, till the Sun has run one third of his course, and disperst all the unwholesome Damps. Then, after Stretching and Yawning for half an Hour, they light their Pipes, and under the Protection of a cloud of Smoak, venture out into the open Air; tho', if it happens to be never so little cold, they quickly return Shivering into the Chimney corner. When the weather is mild, they stand leaning with both their arms upon the corn-field fence, and gravely consider whether they had best go and take a Small Heat at the Hough: but generally find reasons to put it off till another time. Thus they loiter away their Lives, like Solomon's Sluggard, with their Arms across, and at the Winding up of the Year Scarcely have Bread to Eat. (92)

Such an observation could not have been possible without Byrd's having spent long periods of time watching his subjects from before sunup to after sundown, season after season—something we know Byrd could not have done given the limited amount of time he spent in the backwoods.

Lynn points out that Byrd's assigning indolence as motivation for his "lubbers" becomes suspect when he himself confesses to a "lazy" nature (20). In fact, he applies the term "lazy" to the Indians as well, comparing both them and the "lubbers" to the "wild Irish," a comparison his London audience would have especially relished (54, 102). It might further be noted that his model, Petronius, was famous for his idle nature.

The point should also be made that simply existing in a back-woods cabin, particularly in those days, was a backbreaking, never-ending endeavor. Just keeping warm in such a noninsu-lated, naturally cold edifice would have been work indeed in those pre-chain-saw days. In addition, as J. Wayne Flynt notes, "Southern poor whites have always lived by an ethic of repair or mend" where salvage items such as worn-out horseshoes are constantly reworked to function as hinges and other essential items (17). None of this endeavor is, or would have been then, apparent to the passerby or casual observer.[1]

The less-than-human quality Byrd gives to his impoverished characters is evident in the double standard he applies to the classes when he records the sexual exploits of his fellow Virginians. When the objects of their often violent advances are daughters or sisters of plantation owners, Byrd objects to his companions' antics, decrying their having broken "the Rules of Hospitality, by several gross Freedoms they offer'd to take" before Byrd intervenes to save the victims' "chastity." The attempted violations he deems "unhandsome Behavior" (56, 67).

But when the objects of their attractions are of the servant class, Byrd has no such objections, happily reporting episodes such as the following:

I retir'd early to our Camp at some distance from the House, while my Colleagues tarry'd within Doors, & refresh't themselves with a Cheerful Bowl. In the Gaiety of their Hearts, they invited a Tallow-faced Wench that had sprain'd her Wrist to drink with them, and when they had rais'd her in good Humor, they examined all her hidden Charms, and play'd a great many gay Pranks. While Firebrand [a pseudonym Byrd gave to a colleague] who had the most Curiosity, was ranging over her sweet Person, he pick't off several Scabs as big as Nipples, the Consequence of eating too much Pork. The poor Damsel was disabled from making any resistance by the Lameness of her Hand. (59)

Another episode that can easily qualify as rape is recorded with much gaiety:

My landlord had unluckily sold our Men some Brandy, which produced much disorder, making some too Cholerick, and others too loving. So that a Damsel who came to assist in the Kitchen wou'd certainly have been ravish't, if her timely consent had not prevented the Violence. (147-49)

Sadly, Byrd's writings have been taken as literal truth by some, even though, to quote Percy G. Adams in his introduction to the Dover edition, Byrd's "observations" were hardly "scientific." Adams cites two examples to prove his point. One is Byrd's insistence that North Carolina alligators swallow rocks in order to make themselves heavy enough to capture and drag down passing cows and eat them. Another is his statement that eating bear meat not only caused an increase in the birth rate among Indians but was responsible for the "fact" that all of the wives of Byrd's companions gave birth exactly nine months after the return of their husbands. In addition, Adams writes, Byrd's later diaries reveal that he was a "practical joker who, like his contemporary Swift, delighted in putting the 'bite' on someone" (xvi-xviii).

It is too bad that the "bite" has been put on so many readers, and that so much criticism has been devoted to characterizations gleaned from a man who would have laughed uproariously at anyone taking him literally. It is also sad that characterizations invented to satisfy the aristocracy of London who wished to maintain their sense of superiority to Americans should have been relished by those same Americans who supposedly have expurgated such snobbery from their consciousness.

# 3

# William Gilmore Simms:
# The Dispossessed as Villain

Novelist William Gilmore Simms first came to prominence in the late 1830s at about the time Byrd's *History* was published. But while Byrd sought to amuse his audience, Simms sought to enlighten his. Thus where the frontiersman in Byrd is a comic figure, in Simms he's a villain. The difference in the two seems to have stemmed from a difference in the times in which each lived. Byrd saw his subjects grubbing out a subsistence living on their patches of barely tillable soil, perfectly content, he thought, to remain where they were, posing no threat to society as a whole. Simms observed much the same people in harder times, as squatters on the lands of others and as migrants to the west in search of decent land to farm. Mistakenly believing such wanderers had abandoned perfectly good land in the east out of greed, he could only see them as disruptors of an otherwise perfect society.

Simms felt southern society to be a microcosm of the universe with its Great Chain of Being. Each individual, in order to achieve true happiness and harmony, must find his or her place in society and be content to stay there. In the Old South, this meant the planter at the top and the slave at the bottom. In between were various degrees of middle-class society. "Poor whites" were simply misfits, since there was no need in America for poverty to exist in the first place.

It seems strange at first to observe Simms espousing such a viewpoint, since he himself fought to keep his head above water financially for most of his life. He was, to use Jay B. Hubbell's phrase, a "rather aggressive, self-educated merchant's son" who lamented his entire life that he was not accepted by the aristocrats of Charleston society. It is not so strange, however, when we consider that at the time he most forcefully presented his argument in favor of a stratified society with the planter firmly on top, he had only recently married the daughter of a plantation owner and become a member of the planter class. To again quote Hubbell, "from this time on his point of view was somewhat colored by his new connection" (577, 575).

Simms delineates his philosophy most clearly in his early novel *Richard Hurdis* (1838). The story is told from the point of view of the title character who, when he reaches twenty-one, leaves the Alabama plantation of his parents for adventure in the newly opened Choctaw territory, taking with him "a fine horse, a few hundred dollars in specie, three able-bodied negroes, a good rifle," and a friend, William Carrington (15-16).

On the road they encounter a "cavalcade" of migrant families "from one of the poorest parts of North Carolina, bent to better their condition in the western valley, full of dreams." According to Hurdis, they have abandoned their homes in the east for no other reason than that land is cheap on the frontier. As such, they represent "the deterioration of the graces of society," and the longer they wander and the more they associate with the "savage Indians," the worse the deterioration (65, 52).

Hurdis and his entourage ride off, leaving the migrants "in a perfect gale of delighted merriment, having their best wishes, and giving them ours in return." He reasons that, although he himself feels sad about their nomadic situation, the migrants themselves do not. This "race" of people, he decides, have "weak" minds and cannot feel sadness: "On the contrary, they are usually joyful and light spirited enough. It is only in the thoughts and fancies of the spectator that gloom hangs over their path," and this because the spectator recalls the "deserted country which they have left—of the cottage overgrown with weeds." Nor could good fortune help such people. If they ever gain wealth, he says, they are sure to be totally corrupted by it, given that they are "wholly ignorant of its proper uses."

And so the migrants go on their way in "shattered vehicles and bandaged harness," lightheartedly "full of hope and confidence," unaware of their future. "Will their hopes be confirmed?" he asks. "These are doubts which may well make the thoughtful sad." But the wanderers themselves, ignorant in their bliss, do not share the protagonist's doubts and go happily on their way. Thus to the narrator, these people have neither intelligence nor imagination (67).

The two companions next find shelter with a poor family and spend the night in "a miserable hovel" in which they are "clustered together" with their host, his wife, and their children. "The poor wretches" furnish them a hearty supper of bacon, eggs, and hoecake and refuse payment for it. Despite this hospitality, the two men are unable to fathom their host's "cutthroat and hang-dog expression" and they lie all night with pistols at the ready (71).

A character who plays a significant part in the novel is Ben Pickett, a member, we are told, of the "poor and inferior class" and "a burly ruffian . . . rarely clean . . . who had no mode of livelihood, of which the neighbors knew." He is a squatter who steals corn from the planters' fields and coaxes the slaves into stealing cotton and other property and selling it cheaply to him so that he can resell it at a higher price. Even his wife is "sour and dissatisfied. Her looks when not vacant, [are] dark and threatening." Their child, who is "idiot-born," is "pretty, at times seemingly beautiful," but her mind is "utterly lacking." The wife's moral superiority to her husband, we are told, arises from the fact that she knows her place in society as her husband does not, and "is careful to accommodate her conduct and appearance to the well-known humility of condition in which she lived" (83-84).

John Hurdis, who wishes to get rid of his brother Richard, a rival in romance, asks Ben to kill him. Ben gladly consents when he is offered money and goes off happily to hunt down Richard and dispose of him, but not before his wife gives him a sermon on his place in the class structure. The rich and poor have different paths in life, she tells him, and "it's the misfortune of poor people that they're always poking into the wrong path. No wonder the rich despise such people. I despise them myself, though God knows I'm one of the poorest." She explains further: "The poor don't need money. We have no use for it. We want harmony only and homespun" (92-94). She has, we are told in another instance, "character which lifted her, however poor and lowly had been her birth and her station, immeasurably above the base creature [John Hurdis] whose superior wealth had furnished the facilities, and, too frequently in the minds of men, provides a sanction, for the violent abuses of the dependence and inferiority of the poor" (110).

The theme of class separation and the need of all parties to maintain that separation is restated later by Colonel Grafton, whose household reflects the order needed in society as a whole if it is to remain stable. "Everything seems to fit about him," we are told. "Nothing is out of place; and wife, children, servants—all, not only seem to know their special places but to delight in them" (158). After hearing the Colonel's lecture on unsettled people who disrupt the harmony of the whole society by their restless wanderings, the protagonist decides that he himself needs to settle down and return to his father's plantation.

It is from the Colonel also that we hear Simms's ultimate statement on poverty, that no one needs to be poor: "In a country like ours, no man need steal, nor lie, nor cheat. The bread of life is procured with no difficulty by any man having his proportion of limbs and sinews, and not too lazy and vicious for honest employment" (374).

Simms, however, seems to have had a hard time justifying, even to himself, the position of the plantation owner in society, observing, shortly after his marriage, that "to hunt, to ride, to lounge, and to sleep,—perhaps to read a few popular novels conducing to repose—is the sum and substance of our country performances." Sixteen years later he wrote in an essay published in the *Southern Quarterly Review*, "It is a mistake to ascribe the intellectual greatness, or the political success, the eloquence, or the virtues of the south, to agriculture exclusively. Our great men have not been simply planters" (Hubbell 583).

This sentiment seems to have been closer to his true feelings than the reverence for planters and their position in society expressed in *Richard Hardis*. For Simms was, after all, a merchant's son who aspired to be accepted by the aristocracy but felt himself rejected at every turn. Further, he was an early admirer, as had been his father, of Andrew Jackson, and was, in the words of his early biographer, William P. Trent, "a consistent Jeffersonian" throughout his life (60).

This he illustrates most forcefully in *The Forayers* (1885), a novel that appeared a year after the essay. In that novel Colonel Sinclair, "one of the despots of the old school," doesn't feel he needs to earn his right to be a leader. His son Willie feels otherwise and, in fact, marries a member of the merchant class. In a pertinent passage, he gives the Colonel a lesson in Jeffersonian democracy. True aristocrats, he argues, might well come from another class:

There is, here and there, a natural nobility in individuals. . . . There are persons to whom refinement is native—who are born noble, delicate and just in sentiment, magnanimous in soul, generous in courage, endowed with noble talents, and devoted to noble purposes. It is the duty of an aristocracy to acknowledge all such persons, as soon as found, and take them lovingly into their embrace. (86-87)

Such an individual is rare, he maintains, but if an occasional person wishes to rise to the ruling class and is denied entrance, that person acquires low self-esteem and seeks vengeance. Willie, it would appear, is speaking in behalf of the merchant class and not the poor, but in the end, the Colonel, who has earlier objected to his prospective daughter-in-law's "low blood," becomes a convert to this new thinking.

In Eutaw (1856), however, Simms reiterates his original position on the poorest segment of society, creating a spokesman for that segment in the villainous Dick of Tophet ("Hell-Fire Dick") who repeatedly states his dissatisfaction with his societal status. "How is it," he asks at one point, "that one man will git the feed of twenty, and another man won't git his own poor share of one, though he has all the trouble and risk?" He answers his own question with the assertion that "the harrystocracy keeps all the book l'arning to themselves." He then engages in a bit of looking into the future, beyond the Revolutionary War, asking rhetorically, "I wonder, when the fighting's done, how we're to git along." At another point he declares, "The l'arning's the thing . . . ef I only had that, how I'd regilate the country. I'd be king of the cavalries" (248, 269).

The rise to power of the "low" people, however, is not what the narrator has in mind for the betterment of society. He tells us in no uncertain terms that "the self esteem of such a ruffian as Dick of Tophet forbids that he shall come auspiciously in contact with any of the recognized apostles of truth" found in books (259).

Nevertheless, Hell-Fire Dick does eventually borrow a book, Pilgrim's Progress, and compels the boy he is holding captive to read to him. But then he proceeds to get drunk and to fall asleep during the reading, having made no sense of the few words he does hear. The book, which he carries over "his bosom" into battle, saves his life, however, causing him to reflect on "the mysteries of providence" and to decide that there is a God, after all. He even feels remorse for his actions against the boy and now wants to save him from danger, a sentiment he has not experienced before. Shortly thereafter he is killed in battle, having realized that, for him, the value of books is only in their capacity to stop bullets and that he has no business trying to learn to read and rise above his class (272, 552-55).

Meanwhile Willie weds his "low blood" merchant-class wife and lives happily ever after, confirming the extent to which

Simms was willing to extend Jeffersonian principles—namely, only as far down the social scale as the class into which he himself was born. In his defense it should be said that few southerners of his time wanted to extend democracy any further than that.

# 4

## The Southwest Humorists:
## The Dispossessed as Buffoon and Jester

Augustus B. Longstreet had perhaps the most varied career of any American writer. He was a lawyer, judge, newspaper editor, Methodist minister, and president of Emory College, the University of Mississippi, and the University of South Carolina. Born into a respected, if financially troubled, Georgia family, and enamored of wealth and power, he very early adopted, and throughout his life maintained, the conservative philosophy of those politicians with whom he was in constant association.

Along with a firm belief in the rightness of slavery, conservatives in the South held equally to the concept that the lines separating the various classes among whites were nearly as distinct as those separating the races. Nor were they alone in this. The notion was shared by northern conservatives as well. Noah Webster, for example, declared that "the distinction of rich and poor does exist, and must always exist; no human power or device can prevent it" (Schlesinger 20-21). Thus did the threat of universal suffrage in the 1830s convince conservatives nationwide that civilization as they knew it was crumbling all around them.

Conservatives in the South felt a double threat. On the one hand, they dreaded the advent of universal suffrage, which would extend the vote to nonlandholding whites; on the other, they feared the end of slavery, which would free the blacks. Either, taken alone, would dangerously disrupt the social order; together, they threatened utter chaos. Moreover, the old guard could see they would be obsolete in the fast-emerging new order, and as history demonstrates, they were far from wrong. William R. Taylor explains:

Men of a different stripe were receiving the recognition which had once gone to gentlemen of the old school. The result was a generation of

25

highly educated southerners who tended to view changes taking place within the south and the nation with mounting alarm, and to take a tragic view of their own displacement. (14)

Longstreet took it upon himself to argue their case. As for slavery, he quoted both Scripture and the Constitution in its defense. As for universal suffrage, he exposed the "common man" in satiric sketches as a less-than-human grotesque.

Longstreet first gained literary fame outside his region when he sent a copy of his sketches, which he titled *Georgia Scenes,* to Edgar Allan Poe at the *Southern Literary Messenger.* Poe praised the book as an accurate account of "the manners of our South-Western peasantry" (Hubbell 668). Probably because of Poe's recommendation, the book was picked up by a New York publisher and circulated widely. As a result, Longstreet was successful in creating not only his own place in the literary scene but also an entire school of Southwest humorists who were inspired by his narrations of the antics of his "low class" character, Ramsey Sniffle.

Clement Eaton has commented that "to modern eyes the lowest class of whites of the Old South . . . appear to be tragic figures, but to the planters and the residents of the towns they were a comic element." Eaton further sees Longstreet, as well as the other humorists, as "unhampered by European traditions" and thus able to "create a native American humor based on realistic observations" (60-61).

Whether or not we agree on the realism involved, we cannot quarrel with Eaton's assessment that Longstreet sees his lower-class characters as comic and not tragic. The question becomes whether or not we can laugh when he makes fun of such people. For example, do we really enjoy his description of an impoverished "clay eater" who is obviously suffering from the effects of malnutrition, malaria, and hookworm as "a sprout of Richmond" whose early diet of red clay and blackberries has given him "a complexion that a corpse would have disdained to own," and whose "long spells of the fever and ague" as a child "have conspired with clay and blackberries to throw him quite out of the order of nature" (58)?

Further, such a man in actual life would have had to spend a considerable amount of time trying to keep body and soul together, and yet Longstreet's creation spends his time urging acquaintances into fist fights, for, we are told, "there was nothing on earth which delighted Ramsey so much as a fight"—evidently not even a full meal. It is at Ramsey's urging, in fact, that two otherwise peaceable men get into one of the most graphic and bloody fights in the annals of fiction, illustrating Longstreet's taste for violence. He creates for us a scene in which one of his antagonists "hit the ground so hard it jarred his nose off," only to discover that he has "lost his left ear, and a large piece of his left cheek." The other, "a hideous spectacle," emerges with "about a third of his nose . . . bit off and his face so swelled and bruised that it was difficult to discover in it anything of the human visage" (67).

It seems odd that this type of exaggerated writing, which reduces "poor whites" to complete ridicule, has late-twentieth-century advocates. Yet Richard Harwell, in his introduction to a 1975 edition of the work, adds his voice to Eaton's and a host of others by calling it "a forthright picture of frontier Georgia" and an "accurate representation of the people." Longstreet, according to Harwell, "knew the Georgians he described" since "he grew up with them, and he saw them at the courts throughout middle Georgia" (ix, xvii). Such a comment is, of course, based on the assumption that a judge, looking down upon the people brought before him, is seeing them with a completely objective eye and can penetrate their minds to discern motivation for their actions.

The development of the lower-class figure as comic character for political reasons was not an invention of Longstreet, of course. As Kenneth S. Lynn has shown, this phenomenon of southern literature was due to the enormous influence of Sir Walter Scott's novels throughout the South. The aristocrats saw Scott as sympathetic to their view of a stable caste-oriented society, and in his novels, the comic "low" characters function as foils to make the aristocrats "seem more grand by contrast." "Thanks in considerable part to the example of Scott," Lynn concludes, "humor as well as romance was enlisted in the southern cause," serving to reinforce "the point that southern gentlemen stood for law and order, whereas Jacksonian louts represented an all-encompassing anarchy" (54, 192). This concept has proved to be an enduring one in southern fiction and appears as late as Faulkner in his depiction of the "poor white" Snopes clan who invade and ultimately conquer the power structure of Yoknapatawpha County, and by extension, the entire South.

Johnson Jones Hooper's chief literary creation is the dishonest, lazy, and unprincipled title character of *Some Adventures of Simon Suggs* (1844). Suggs's "whole ethical system," we are told early in that volume, "lies snugly in his favourite aphorism—'it is good to be shifty in a new country'—which means it is right and proper that one should live as merrily and as comfortably as possible at the expense of others." He is a "miracle of shrewdness" with a "quick, ready wit" and the ability to "detect the soft spots in his fellow, and to assimilate himself to whatever company he may fall in with" (8-10). Such a character can easily be seen as an earlier version of Flem Snopes who, as Cecil D. Elby notes, is "cut from the same cloth" (18).

Some of Hooper's admirers have sought to point out his reliability as an objective observer. Manly Wade Wellman, for example, in his 1969 introduction to the Chapel Hill reissue of the text, dismisses two earlier documented arguments—one by Robert Hopkins that Suggs was a caricature of Andrew Jackson, and another by Walter Blair that Hooper was influenced by the European picaresque novel. Wellman substitutes instead his own theory that Hooper's "inspiration must have been gained, in large part, at first hand" (xvii). And Paul Somers, Jr., who also defends Hooper's objectivity, has this to say about the poor white "dirt eaters" that Hooper satirizes: "They were not especially dishonest—perhaps that required too much effort—just poorly educated, they seemed to prove that some people would manage to fail anywhere" (5).

Somers does, however, differ with Wellman in seeing Hooper's sketches as being politically motivated. He presents, in fact, a strong defense of Hopkins's thesis that *Simon Suggs* is "a direct burlesque of political biographies of Andrew Jackson" (28). It is difficult indeed to imagine anyone who reads Somers's account being afterward convinced by those critics who, like McIlwaine, argue that the goal of Hooper and the other Southwest humorists was simply "to record types and manners and to amuse" (41). Few men living in those times were apolitical, and anyone with Hooper's convictions could not have kept his views out of any writing he did, much less writing that depicted the "common man" whose rise to power Hooper and his fellow conservatives so greatly feared.

George Washington Harris's *Sut Lovingood* (1867) has as its title character "a queer-looking, long legged, short-bodied, small-headed, white-haired, hog-eyed, funny sort of genius" who rides into town on a "nick-tailed, low-necked, long poor, pale sorrel horse" to chat with a crowd of mountaineers depicted as "full of fun, foolery, and mean whiskey" (34). The rest of the book consists of tales told by Sut himself.

We are not long into the tales before we learn that what Sut tells us about himself is true—that he relishes inflicting pain on his fellow creatures, a trait he attributes to "unregenerate human nature." Moreover, he tells us, we all share his feelings on this if we would only admit it. For example, once we have done something harmful to someone without cause, we are bound to hate that person always and want to "hurt em agin" (137).

Sut especially likes the idea of physically abusing young animals and human babies, particularly when they are about ready to nurse at their mother's breast. This, too, he attributes to "human nature" and asks the reader if it isn't really true that "when you sees a little long legged lamb" staggering under its mother "a-huntin for the tit," your desire is to seize him by the tail and fling him "over the fence among the blackberry briars?" Or, spotting a little calf doing the same thing, "dont you want to kick hit on the snout, hard enough to send hit backwards, say fifteen foot." Finally, upon seeing a baby "a-snifflin after the breast," while its mother struggles to "git hit out, over the hem of her clothes, don't you feel hungry to give hit just one percussion cap slap" to show it that it can't be fed everytime it gets hungry (138-39).

Grownups are another matter. Sut implies that we don't want to slap them; instead our overwhelming desire is to kick him or her as hard as a mule kicks, simply "for the way they wears their hat, or watch-chain; the shape of their nose; the cut of their eye; or somethin of the like nature" (138-39). Granted, this is a tormented soul, and may reflect the author's torment, but to laugh with Sut one would have to share, at least in part, his desires.

Harris's caricatures of "poor whites" become most offensive when he pictures Sut's family, who appear to be at near-starvation status and yet enjoy life to the fullest, in the vein of Ramsey Sniffle and other "rogues" created by authors who never faced abject poverty themselves. And in a manner that looks forward to Erskine Caldwell, Harris reduces his "poor white trash" to the status of animals.

This is particular!y evident in the first story when Sut relates how the family's one horse has died and they are left "without ary hoss to crop with." Sut's father, whom Sut describes as "daddratted mean and lazy and savage," lies awake one night "a-snortin, and rollin, and blowin, and shufflin, and scratchin hisself." The next morning he gleefully volunteers to substitute for the dead animal. Sut rigs up an umbrella brace for a brid!e and attaches it to his father who proceeds to behave in strict animal fashion:

When we got the bridle fixed onto Dad, don't you b'lieve he set in to chompin it just like a real hoss and tried to bite me on the arm. . . . While Mam were a-tyin the belly band . . . he dropped onto his hands, said 'Whay-a-a' like a mad hoss would, and slung his hind legs at Mam's head. . . . He just run back'ards on all fours and kicked at her agin—and pawed the ground with his fists. (7)

As they plow, Dad responds to Sut's tongue-clucking, "leanin for'ard o his pullin . . . same as a real hoss" until he charges into a hornet's nest and lights out, clearing the bushes "with a squeal," and proceeds to jump from the top of a bluff twenty-five feet down to the water, where he bobs up and down trying unsuccessfully to free himself from the hornets, all of which Sut finds hilarious (7-9).

In another passage that looks forward to later writers, including Faulkner, who find humor in dead bodies and grotesque female characters, Sut is given the task of burying "Missis Yardley," a local widow, "fixin her for rottin comfortably" and "coverin her up with soil to keep the buzzards from cheatin the worms." The widow, it seems, has died after "she got a scared hoss to run over her." Her daughter is "built at first 'bout the length of her arm, but were never stretched any by a pair of steers," with the result that she is "fat enough to kill." Sut blames his own hump-back on "a-stoopin to kiss that squatty lard-stand of a gal" (171-74).

Sut compounds his degrading picture of women—and African-Americans—with a description of a young girl's breasts as "two snow balls with a strawberry stuck butt ended into both of 'em" and her hair as black as a "nigger handlin charcoal" (35-36). He adds this animalistic description: "Did you ever notice . . . at all social gatherings when the he's begin to gather, that the young she's begin to tickle one another and the ole maids swell their tails, roach up their backs, sharpen their nails into the bedposts and door jambs, and spit and groan sorta like cats a-courtin?" These "ole maids," he tells us, can be reduced to purring if you get one alone and show her who's in charge by giving her "a tetch of the bridle" (177-78).

Given passages such as these, it is difficult to take seriously a respected critic who writes that Sut's characterization is "undoubtedly true to life" and that "the squalor in which the Lovingoods live—squalor without alleviation, without shame—somehow becomes very jolly" (Blair 91, 101). Or another who tells us that Sut is simply "a rough but good-natured Tennessee mountaineer . . . [whose] comic—and often bawdy—situations are invariably underlined by a homely but sound philosophy" (Beatty et al. 398). Or yet another who insists that, although "cruelty (especially towards the Negro and foreigners) abounds" in the works of the Southwest humorists, their humor can be defended on the ground that it is "masculine" (Inge 138).

One is more apt to agree with Edmund Wilson's comment that *Sut Lovingood* is a "repellent book" and Sut himself "avowedly sadistic" (509), even though such agreement, in the eyes of many of Harris's defenders, renders one unappreciative of "American humor." Brom Weber, for example, dismisses Wilson's criticism by placing him in the "genteel tradition" that demands that humor be "wholly benevolent and compassionate." Such a view, Weber says, is basically sentimental and more British than American (49-50). When we combine this charge that Wilson is not American enough with the notion that it is masculine to enjoy Sut's humor, one can readily see why few critics have come to Wilson's defense.

Readers of *Sut Lovingood* can't say they haven't been warned, however. Sut himself, in his introductory remarks, tells us to be on guard. "If you is feard of smut," he says, "don't climb the chimney" (xxxii). Although Harris is no doubt seeking to head off adverse criticism of his humor by categorizing his critics as prudes, Sut's advice is well worth taking, for it is difficult to find a reason other than historical to read any of the Southwest humorists at this late date.

These writers, in the words of Lewis P. Simpson, present a vision that, in the end, is pessimistic because it entails a fear of "the arrival of democratic man on the stage of world history" (62). As such, it is disconcerting to have their humor presented to us as the dominant American type. Indeed, since the American experience has been the gradual extension of democracy to all, it would seem that their humor is more aberrant than representative.

# Part Two:

# Lessening the Stereotype

# 5

# The New South and the Forgotten People

During the Civil War, the various classes of the South were brought together through sheer circumstance, creating what many editorialists in the postwar period believed was a democratic spirit engendered by a common cause. Others of a more conservative persuasion felt the war proved the social order that had existed in the Old South was valid, that the aristocrats, as officers, had proven themselves worthy of the top spot in the hierarchy through bravery, endurance, and leadership, and that the lower classes had been happy to follow their lead. This view was promoted as late as 1962 by historian Richard M. Weaver (246-53).

Neither theory, however, proved to be right. Bell Irvin Wiley, through research into contemporary sources, uncovered a great deal of resentment and bitterness during the war on the part of the poor toward the aristocrats. This, he says, was due to two primary causes: the law that exempted owners of twenty slaves or more from military service, and the exempted slaveowners' habit of hoarding foodstuffs while the wives and children of conscripted poor farmers were on the verge of starvation. One such wife was prompted to complain that her husband was fighting for nothing except "for his family to starve" (64-68).

Nonetheless, a number of southerners, no doubt looking for signs of hope in those devastating years after the war, got themselves to believe not only that a democratic leveling had taken place during the war but that the war's aftermath had actually created an "economic democracy" in which the plantation system had broken down into a "New Order"—a process Sidney Lanier called the "quiet rise of the small farms." Supposedly these farms were happily tended, not by "poor whites," but rather by that picturesque figure celebrated by later southern apologists, the "yeoman farmer."

But, as C. Vann Woodward has pointed out, this rosy picture of a new Jeffersonian democracy was more myth than reality. In truth, "the evils of land monopoly, absentee ownership, soil mining, and a one-crop system, once associated with and blamed upon slavery, did not disappear with that institution, but were, instead, aggravated, intensified, and multiplied." What emerged after the war was a "lien system" in which the merchant replaced the planter as chief landholder. The merchants gave the small farmers credit against future crops, and in the process, the farmers became more and more indebted to the merchants. In such a system, the supposedly "contented" small farmers became increasingly "wretched" (*Origins* 175-80).

Many, of course, saw this wretchedness and began to call for a reassessment of the agrarian system. Some called for a full-fledged Yankee-style industrialization of the entire South. Leading these proponents of a "New South" was Henry W. Grady of the *Atlanta Constitution*. He saw the problem as one of southerners not taking advantage of natural resources all around them:

No people ever held larger stewardship than the people of the South. It is theirs to produce and enlarge the crop of that staple that largely clothes the world. It is theirs to conserve and develop the final and fullest supply of coal and iron, and to furnish from their enormous forests the lumber and hard woods to meet the world's demands. (145)

Widespread industrialization, however, was not to help the poor either. In fact, northern industrialists who came south in droves adapted readily to the social system already in place, fashioning what Simkins has called a "new feudalism resembling that which had existed under slavery," building fine houses for themselves while placing their workers "in villages that resembled the slave quarters of old" (10, 372).

The workers were, by and large, failed tenant farmers and sharecroppers who could not make a living on the land, having become victims of the lien system. One of them put it this way: "Mr. Johnson, my landlord, got half of [the crop] because the land was his'n, and he took the other half to pay for what rashins he'd furnished." This particular tenant farmer explained that "after the landlord had taken all of his possessions, including his last pig, he and his family were forced to give up and go to work in the mill" (Newby, *Plain Folk* 1).

Not only did the industrialists maintain the feudalism through building "company towns"—a pattern followed by John D. Rockefeller and others in western coal towns as well—they also adopted the assumption that planters had made regarding their slaves, that they were "benefactors," saving the poor from a life of extreme depravation and providing for their needs with low-paying jobs, low-rent housing, and a company store. They saw themselves, in effect, as taking care of the workers, maintaining the paternalistic system that had been put into place by the plantation owners in the Old South.

Frank Tannenbaum, a northerner who traveled through the South in the early 1920s, heard the philosophy behind this system from an unexpected source—a professor, who, after praising the mill workers in a nearby town for being industrious, went on to inform his visitor that the workers were actually "like children, and we have to take care of them." In exchange for this "benevolence," the workers agreed that they would not seek to supplement their income by finding additional work elsewhere, and that when their children came to be of working age, they would not look for better paying jobs in other places (40-46).

Under such a system, it is no wonder that the mill workers were unhappy. Barely making a living, and called "lintheads" by their more prosperous neighbors, they and their counterparts across the South vented their frustration in hatred of the newly freed African-Americans who were their competitors for menial jobs. Having lost all sense of self-worth, and at the same time living in a society that measured self-worth by one's status in the hierarchy, "poor whites" could only feel a part of the human race by believing there were some below even them. As James McBride Dabbs explains: "Under slavery, the only thing that distinguished the 'poor whites,' so-called, from the slaves was that the former had the prestige of being white and free. Now they had only the prestige of being white, and doubtless they clung fiercely to it" (104).

With the merchants and industrialists in economic control and the old aristocracy back in political control after the failure of Reconstruction, the poor of both races were locked into poverty. Nor did the situation improve over the years, leading an Alabamian to declare in 1924 that "the great masses of whites and colored citizens of the Southern states . . . are held in political and economic serfdom" (Skaggs x). Early advocates of a New South, such as Grady, didn't help matters much either, for they were, by and large, laissez-faire capitalists who believed that the lot of the poor would of necessity improve with increasing industrialization.

Not all southerners were blind to the plight of the poor, however, for as George B. Tindall notes, "[A] substantial minority of southerners [in the postwar South] belonged to the social justice wing of progressives who looked beyond the loosening of economic restriction to positive action against social ills" (10).

One such man was Walter Hines Page, a newspaper editor in Raleigh, North Carolina, who, frustrated by the South's resistance to change, moved north to establish Doubleday, Page, and Company, which published southern writers such as Ellen Glasgow and Booker T. Washington. It was from there that he issued his most serious indictments of the South. He also served on President Theodore Roosevelt's Commission on Country Life in 1908 and on the Rockefeller Sanitary Commission for the Eradication of Hookworm Disease in 1909, helping to establish dispensaries for treatment throughout the southern states.

Page's main remedy for poverty, however, lay in educating the poor. Using the phrase "the forgotten man" to describe the disadvantaged whites of the South, a phrase Franklin D. Roosevelt was to apply thirty years later to poor people all across America, he wrote:

The old system of class education . . . did not touch the masses. They grew up with the idea that education was a special privilege: they did not aspire to it, did not believe that it was attainable, and at last they came to believe that it was not desirable, certainly that it was not necessary. They remained illiterate, neglected, forgotten. (15)

"In his ignorance," Page continues, "the forgotten man was content to be forgotten." Told by politicians to be wary of higher taxes which could have paid for his children's education, and counseled by preachers that "God meant his poverty as a means of grace," he became "thankful for being neglected" (22-23).

Page further argued that "the forgotten man" constituted a majority of the people of the South and that while keeping most of the population uneducated may have suited the few on top, it prevented the entire region from progressing beyond a state of "backwardness." For this reason, the South produced no first-rate universities or libraries. The whole of society suffered, in effect, because the capabilities of a vast majority of the people languished untapped. Echoing the Jeffersonian principle that the ability to learn is not limited to the upper class, Page called for widespread public education to provide "equality of opportunity." "You can never judge a man's capacity," he wrote, "except as he has opportunity to develop it." Giving that opportunity to only the ruling class had badly hampered the South while the rest of the nation, which sought to educate a larger group of its citizens, progressed intellectually and materially, "making more rapid conquests . . . than in any preceding time in the history of the world" (5, 19).

But to achieve anything approximating that kind of prosperity, Page maintained, the South needed to get over its deep-seated fear of change and, most important, of taxation, for that was the only method by which funds could be raised to build public schools. "It was a misfortune for us," he wrote, "that the quarrel with King George happened to turn on a question of taxation—so great was the dread of taxation that was instilled into us." If the South did not overcome that dread, he concluded, it would solidify itself in perpetual ignorance and poverty (12).

Edwin Anderson Alderman was an educator of the same period who also campaigned for public schools in the South. At one time president of Tulane University and later of the University of Virginia, he reinforced Page's call for reform. "Education in democracies," he wrote, "is not a question of philanthropy, or expediency, but of life and death" (517).

Over thirty years later, sociologist Howard W. Odum, who taught in rural Mississippi and later at Columbia University and the University of North Carolina, voiced the same sentiments, maintaining, in 1936, that the South was still a "backward" region. He also echoed Page and Alderman in declaring that the lack of an "adequate system of universal education with the strict enforcement of compulsory attendance laws was a greater cause of southern waste of resources than were farming methods." Odum advocated regional planning along with public education as a way out of the South's "backwardness" (4:15).

Page, Alderman, and Odum were, of course, denounced in their own times as traitors to the South, as were others who agreed with them. Nonetheless, their voices were heard. And their essential message of universal education and equality of opportunity remains a mainstay of southern, as well as northern, liberalism to this day. In addition, their ideas were shared by a number of authors of the late nineteenth and early twentieth centuries who, in contrast to the writers preceding them, sought to depict disadvantaged whites not as stereotypes but as human beings.

# 6

## Joel Chandler Harris:
## The Dispossessed as Tragic Figure

Joel Chandler Harris described himself as born "under the humblest of circumstances." The son of an Irish day laborer who refused to marry Harris's mother and deserted her soon after the child was born, Joel was keenly aware all of his life of his illegitimacy and the humiliation of having to live his childhood in a one-room cabin donated by a charitable citizen of the town.

His mother, known to the town as Miss Mary, raised her son alone, except for the brief period when her mother came to live with them, and barely made a living as a seamstress. Just how close they came to dire poverty is debatable, for Harris later remembered the townspeople as charitable. "It is a great blessing for a young fellow in the clutches of poverty," he wrote in 1900, "to be raised among such people as those who lived in Eatonton when I was a boy." He noted the "kindly interest" which the townspeople "took in my welfare." Despite his gratitude, however, young Joel suffered the humiliation of being dependent on the charity of others, and this, coupled with the knowledge of his illegitimacy, was a probable cause of his developing a pathological shyness and stammer that he was never able to overcome (Cousins 21-22).

Because of his background, Harris identified strongly with all the downtrodden of the South, wondering in his childhood copybook which was more respectable, being black or "poor folks" (Flusche 175). He was to spend much of his adult life seeking to give dignity to both in his writing. The African-American portrayals are widely known, the "poor white" somewhat less, although his sympathy with the latter ran equally deep. A fair and accurate portrait of the unfortunate "Georgia cracker" was, in fact, a chief aim in his writing, as he noted in an article he wrote for a Chicago publication in 1884:

The American character is seen and known at its best in rural regions; but it is a fatal weakness of American literature that our novelists and story-tellers can perceive only the comic side of what they are pleased to term "provincial life"; for it is always a fatal weakness to see what is not to be seen. It is a remarkable fact that the most characteristic American story that has thus far been written should approach rural life on the tragic side. (qtd. in Julia Collier Harris 204-05)

Harris was speaking specifically of a story by E.W. Howe, but he was also clearly setting his own criteria for literature, for he himself created both comic and tragic characters with irony and sympathy. For Harris, unlike the Southwest humorists, found that sympathy was not difficult.

One illustration of his sympathetic treatment of "poor whites" is the title story in his *Mingo and Other Sketches* (1884). In it he creates Mrs. Feratia Bivins, a "poor white" who is given to bitterly comic tirades against those people she perceives as her enemies, in particular Emily Wornum, an aristocrat who has snubbed her. The anger stems from "the pent up rage of a century" due to "real or fancied wrongs" against her class (212). Harris's sympathy is apparent in his description of the woman, which reveals her essential dignity: "She had thin gray hair, a prominent nose, firm thin lips, and eyes that gave a keen and sparkling individuality to sharp and homely features. She had evidently seen sorrow and defied it. There was no suggestion of compromise in manner or expression" (12-13).

What raises the ire of Mrs. Bivins is the situation in which she finds herself. Her son had earlier married the daughter of the aristocratic Miss Emily, but both her son and her daughter-in-law have since died, leaving their young child in Mrs. Bivins's charge. Years pass and suddenly Miss Emily appears and wants to see her granddaughter. This sends Mrs. Bivins into a rage because Miss Emily has long before disowned her daughter for marrying "beneath" her, not even coming to see the girl when she was dying. "Things is come to a mighty purty pass," she says, "when *quality* folks has to go from house to house a-huntin' up *pore white trash,* an' a-askin airter the'r kin" (21).

Mrs. Bivins delivers this outburst in a "tone . . . husky with suppressed fury; its rage would have stormed the barriers of the grave." And yet, in spite of her desire to physically assault the woman, she restrains her anger because she is able to see "a tender place in that pore mizerbul creetur's soul-case."

Mingo, the African-American who helps Mrs. Bivins around the place, explains to the narrator, "I spec' it seem sorter funny ter you, boss, but dat w'ite 'oman done had lots er trouble; she done had bun'ance er trouble—she sholy *is*" (24-26). Clearly Mingo knows he is speaking to an outsider who needs educating.

Another memorable disadvantaged white character appears in "At Teague Poteet's," a story from the same collection. Teague is of French descent, "a man of marked shrewdness and commonsense" who moves to Hog Mountain among the other "poor whites," sharing their alienation from the more prosperous townspeople, who laugh at his new bride, using epithets like "shiftless" to describe her. Despite being "cut to the quick," he doesn't retaliate because of the "latent pride of his class" (43-46).

When war comes, Teague refuses to fight for the "restercrats'" right to own slaves, since he himself "hain't got none." He further reveals common sense and sensitivity when he tells his "radiantly beautiful" daughter to ignore the taunts of her fellow schoolmates who make fun of her clothes. "Hatin'," he tells her, "is a mighty ha'sh disease." Meanwhile, he goes into the moonshine business so that he can buy her some new dresses (49-50, 132, 74).

Unfortunately, the story that is set up as tragedy—when a revenuer comes to town to destroy Teague's still and falls in love with his daughter—dissolves into sentimentality. What is revealed throughout, however, is Harris's strong feeling about disadvantaged whites and his wish to portray them as human beings with pride and dignity, instead of as the butt of jokes, which he saw in much of the available literature of his time.

Another collection, *Free Joe and Other Georgia Sketches* (1887), contains the story "Free Joe and the Rest of the World," a sympathetic treatment of an unfortunate slave who was freed in 1840, but who now roams the countryside, "an exile," despised by the slaves and feared by the whites. In such a climate, Joe can find only two people who will befriend him, Micajay Staley and his sister, Becky, who live in a cabin next to the plantation where Joe's wife is still a slave. Although he would have earlier scorned the Staleys as "poor white trash," he now seeks their friendship, since they allow him to sit on their back step or under a poplar tree on their land and listen to the slaves singing on the plantation. They also are able to pass along to him information they get about his wife.

One piece of information they learn but refuse to tell him is that his wife has been sold by the plantation owner and that Joe will never see her again. Thus we are set up again for tragic irony which turns into sentimentality instead when the old couple find Joe dead beneath the poplar, still waiting for his wife to appear at the fence.

But the story, however flawed, is readable and moving. Further, it is an excellent example of Harris's working out two themes—the plight of the freed slave who is not really "free," and the capacity of disadvantaged whites for sensitivity and generosity, traits too often denied them by other writers.

The Hightower family in "Trouble on Lost Mountain" also break the stereotype. Viewed as "quaint" by a land-buyer from Boston, they surprise him by treating him with hospitality. Tragedy ensues as a jealous local man, who is in love with the Hightower girl, accidentally kills her as he aims for the newcomer he suspects is his rival. Harris once more evokes a sense of irony that borders on tragedy in much the same way Erskine Caldwell was to do some fifty years later in some of his stories and novels.

"Azabia," a story from the same collection, pointedly depicts the negative stereotyping of "poor whites" that middle-class citizens so often engage in. Emma Jane Stucky, on the verge of starvation, is reduced to begging for herself and her mentally retarded son, Bud. When she enters the Haley Tavern, Mrs. Haley generously gives her food, but cautions her customers to ignore Emma Jane as she is just one of a hundred "pineywoods tackies" who will pester them to no end if they begin to feel pity. Then, in an immediate defensive posture, she hastens to add, "I ain't prejudiced agin the poor creetur'—the Lord knows I ain't" (180-81).

Harris proceeds to show us Emma Jane returning home to her "squalid" house and to her waiting son, who seems "to embody the mute, pent-up distress of whole generations." When he dies of a fever, a Bostonian, Miss Helen, visits, but she is resented by Emma Jane who tells her that when Bud was alive "you wouldn't a-wiped your feet on 'im" (183, 234).

The remarkable thing about this story is that Harris does not once lose sympathy for any of the participants—Mrs. Haley, Miss Helen, Bud, or Emma Jane. It is as if they are all caught in a class system that no one likes but no one can do anything about.

"Mom Bi," a story in *Balaam and his Master* (1891), shows the frustrations and alienation of the African-American just before, during, and after the Civil War. Mom Bi is a house servant who is openly defiant, "her manner . . . abrupt, and her tongue sharp." While she spares no one, she is especially contemptuous of the "sandhillers" who market "their poor little crops in and around the village." She is happy to have been born black, she says, otherwise "I mought born lak some deze white folks what eat dirt un set in de chimerly-corner tell dee look lak dee bin smoke-dried" (172-76).

What most offends her about these "tackies" is that when they are urged by the town to join the Confederate army, they dutifully join up, although it isn't their fight. "What dem po' white trash gwine fight fer?" she asks. "Dee ain't bin had no nigger; dee ain't bin had no money; dee ain't been had no lan'; dee ain't bin had nuttin' 't all" (180).

Mom Bi never forgives the "sandhillers" for marching off to this fight that isn't theirs, but she also objects violently when her owner sends his only son into battle, for this again is wasting a life. What emerges is not only a powerful antiwar statement, but a depiction of two aspects of southern life ignored by others—the bitterness and defiance of the African-American and the unjust use of the "poor white" by his "superiors."

Harris is not a great writer. He too often intrudes upon his stories to preach. And he is obviously sentimental, although much more so in the earlier stories than in the later ones. But he hardly deserves the charge made by Shields McIlwain that he gets "misty-eyed over Cracker halfwits," principally because such criticism is directed more toward Harris's subjects than it is to Harris. Perhaps it is better to see Harris's sentimentality as an overcompensation for the scorn he saw being constantly cast upon an unfortunate group of people. If being sympathetic to the have-nots is a flaw, then Harris is certainly guilty.

# 7

# George Washington Cable:
## The Dispossessed as Benefactor

Unlike Harris, George Washington Cable could lay claim to an aristocratic heritage in that his paternal grandfather had owned slaves in Virginia. But he became, if anything, even more liberal in outlook than Harris, a trait he could also claim as a heritage—and from the same source, for his grandfather had freed his slaves and moved from Virginia to Indiana.

There is another similarity in the lives of the two writers. Cable, like Harris, was left without a father at a young age and grew up in poverty, although in his case there was no benefactor, and he was forced to leave school at the age of fourteen to work in a customs warehouse and later as a clerk for cotton merchants.

Cable's *Dr. Sevier* (1884), his second novel, has been seen almost from the beginning, as a failure. It is not a novel one picks up and reads for enjoyment, for the characters are flat and the episodes contrived. But it is worth looking at for the way Cable points to the existence of poverty in the midst of wealth.

Dr. Sevier is a physician who, along with his private practice, voluntarily works in a ward at Charity Hospital. Passing the cotton exchange on his way to the hospital, he is repulsed by the "semi-respectable larceny" that goes on inside by people who don't seem to care that extreme poverty exists only a few blocks away.

Dr. Sevier, however, blames the poor for their condition, feeling that employment is readily available for anyone who wants to work. The narrator is quick to point out that the doctor is basically a kind man whose ignorance in this area is his never having "known want" (8-9, 98).

Dr. Sevier is thus set up to learn a truth, and he does so by noting the unsanitary conditions in which the poor must live—"the common dumping ground and cesspool of the city"—and by treating their constant bouts with malaria and consumption. He also gains insight when he witnesses the descent into seemingly hopeless poverty of a young man, John Richling. Born of aristocratic Kentucky parents who have disowned him, John comes to New Orleans with his wife, but although he walks the streets looking for work "from daylight to dark," John can find only occasional odd jobs. His problem is that because of his aristocratic background, he has no saleable skills, which, of course, puts him in the same position as the poorest of the poor (101, 113).

And yet when the doctor tries to help the couple with an offer of money, John rejects his charity as a matter of self-respect. This the doctor cannot understand and he harbors "ill-defined anger" toward them, seeking "some shortcoming of theirs" that he can blame for their helplessness, wanting to alleviate his guilt feelings about their condition (136-37, 143, 155).

All the while Dr. Sevier is being sensitized to the realities of poverty, he keeps hearing statements from the prosperous segment of society to the effect that the poor have their "station" and that, after all, they don't feel as deeply as others and thus aren't really suffering to the extent one might think they are. Besides, their poverty has been brought about by the "deficiency of inner resources or character" and, for this reason, the rest of the population need not waste sympathy on them. The trouble with such comments for the doctor is that they remind him of statements he himself has often made and thus make him feel even more troubled (189-90).

The doctor, however, doesn't see the full reality of John's situation and advises him to remember that he is a member of the aristocracy and that he should be seeking employment befitting his "station" instead of asking for menial work that is "beneath" someone of his class. Here, Cable seems to be stretching his point, for any reasonably intelligent person could see that John can't find a job—especially not a position "befitting his station"—because he has no training. But Cable obviously wants us to know the good doctor is still in the process of learning (237-40).

Fortunately John doesn't take Dr. Sevier's advice and goes to work for a baker, which completes his education in matters concerning Cable's theme, and he writes the doctor that he now knows fully "what the poor suffer." Once a "brother to the rich," he has now learned to be "a brother to the poor" (250). Dr. Sevier, who at this point has also learned what he needs to know, advises John to put his newfound wisdom to work to aid the poor, giving a final speech in favor of causes Cable so fervently believed in—

decent housing and job training for the poor, sanitary conditions in the workplace, better hospitals and prisons, and true justice in the courts (292-93). When John falls ill and dies, the doctor talks his widow into working toward bettering the lives of the poor. Work with the rich also, he tells her, get them to realize that it is in their best interest to alleviate poverty conditions. She agrees to take the job and the novel ends happily with the two working together for the betterment of society, rich and poor.

Louis Rubin objects to the novel, not only because it is sermonizing—a valid point—but because he feels that Cable's purpose is unclear. What are we to make of John Richling, he asks? After all, isn't he simply a young man who "cannot enter into the spirit of money making and of getting ahead . . . so he fails and eventually dies. But why? The reason is obscure. Richling does not scorn trade . . . he merely fails to fit in and to prosper, presumably because of his personality." Rubin looks to Cable's life and sees the confusion in Cable's unwillingness to see what it was that made him so discontented in New Orleans society. Rubin maintains that it was the citizens' ignorance about racial matters and concludes that the novel fails because it "says nothing whatever about the Negro issue" (*George W. Cable* 139-44).

What Rubin does not take into account is that Cable was angry about a number of issues, not only racial injustice. His dissatisfaction with New Orleans society stemmed from its disregard of disadvantaged whites as well as its mistreatment of African-Americans. And while it is true, as Rubin so aptly demonstrates, that the people of New Orleans made Cable feel unwelcome principally because he was so liberal on matters of race, we might also suspect that his comments on the situation of the poor—which call into question the whole caste structure of the time and accuse the more prominent citizens of being callous toward a deserving group—couldn't have made him popular either.

This isn't to say the novel succeeds, however. As Rubin notes, Cable's elaborate sermonizing is indeed a flaw; it gets in the way of the narrative and diminishes the drama. But it is certainly understandable, given the extent to which society was ignorant of the effects of poverty. Cable's friend Harris can be accused of oversermonizing on this point also.

Cable, however, has a larger problem in that in *Dr. Sevier* he is trying to do two things at once—to explain the experience of poverty from the perspective of both the "accidental" poor and, at the same time, of the generational poor, and all this through one character, John Richling. Cable's mistake was in not only giving Richling the motivation an aristocrat would have rightly had—the reluctance to ask for employment, the realization that he doesn't have "the art of finding work" because he "was always to be the master and never servant" (448)—but he adds to these the recalcitrant pride of the alien poor when John refuses to take the doctor's financial assistance. Thus Cable's overall understanding of the complexity of the problem leads him to try to do too much explaining with too little material and ultimately to make *Dr. Sevier* a less than satisfactory novel.

*Bonaventure* (1887) is less unified than *Dr. Sevier*, it is three separate stories of Acadian culture that were meant to work together better than they actually do. But while the earlier work contains flat characters, the characters in *Bonaventure* are rounded in a picturesque way, leading one to conclude that Cable has more fondness for them than for either the doctor or John Richling. But, once again, Cable is writing a moral tale about serving others as the way to personal happiness.

Bonaventure Deschamps is a young Creole orphan adopted by an Acadian couple who have a daughter two years older than he is. The first story, "Caranco," is about Bonaventure's unrequited love for her and his part in sending the young man she is interested in off to war.

When the young man returns and marries her, Bonaventure is free to pursue a Christ-like life of self-sacrifice and service to others. He is encouraged to do this by a priest who serves as his mentor in much the same way Preacher Casy serves as Tom Joad's mentor in *The Grapes of Wrath*. In fact, Casy's statement to Tom that everyone is part of "one big soul" echoes these words of the priest to Bonaventure:

God's image makes us so large that we cannot live within ourselves . . . and because in my poor small way I am made like Him, the whole world becomes a part of me. He bound the whole human family together by putting everyone's happiness into some other one's hands. (37)

The second story, "Grande Pointe," relates Bonaventure's becoming a schoolteacher and mentor to a young boy, Claude, to whom he passes along the priest's philosophy of the interconnection of all human beings, adding that all lives are of equal worth, even the "lowliest." To establish that society is badly in need of this lesson, Cable has Mr. Tarbox ride in from the outside world and smugly proclaim, with little more than a glance, that the Acadians are "shiftless." Cable, echoing Harris, makes the additional point that people at the bottom of a stratified society need to feel someone is lower than they are, by having an African-American character say of the "Cajuns," "Dey a lil bit slow" (76).

But the narrator sees a reason for the Acadians' "backwardness":

In France their race had been peasants; in Acadia forsaken colonists . . . and for just one century in Louisiana . . . had been held down by the triple fetter of illiteracy, poverty, and the competition of the unpaid . . . slaves. . . . now the slave was free, the school was free, and a new, wide, golden future waited only on their education. (215)

And thus it is Bonaventure's goal in life to teach the children English so that they can function in American society instead of continuing to be "strangers in the world." The parents, resisting change in typical human fashion, object, and it is up to Bonaventure to convince them, which he does.

Cable further aligns himself with Harris in pointing out the irony and unfairness of "poor whites" fighting what was essentially a rich man's war:

Far away in Virginia, Tennessee, Georgia, on bloody fields, many an Acadian volunteer and many a poor conscript fought and fell for a cause that was really none of theirs, simple, non-slaveholding peasants; and many died in camp and hospital—often of wounds, often of fever, often of mere longing for home. (9)

To the Acadians in the bayous of Louisiana, the two sides in the war were equally destructive of their lives: "The blue meant invasion and the gray meant conscription" (15).

Rubin's assessment of *Bonaventure* is that it is sentimental melodrama, though there is much good description and characterization. Here again it is hard to disagree. But when he further maintains that Cable admired the Acadian's "simplicity and rustic ways though he deplored their conservatism and backwardness and was appalled by their illiteracy" (192), the statement needs to be tempered by a reference to Cable's larger understanding of the nature of poverty and the reasons of illiteracy and obstinacy. Impatient with conservatism, yes. Appalled by illiteracy, yes. But here and elsewhere Cable is careful to point out that the poor's "backwardness" has been forced upon them by conditions they were powerless to control and he maintains that it is the duty of society to realize this. Everyone's life is sacred, he tells us, and it is a waste and an injustice to allow so much as one person to remain in ignorance and poverty when we have the means to bring him or her out of it. This is Cable's message, and he says it loud and clear.

# 8

# Kate Chopin:
# The Dispossessed as Childlike Adult

Chopin was born Catherine O'Flaherty in St. Louis, Missouri. Her father, a prosperous Irish-American merchant, died when she was five years old. Her mother was descended from two of the oldest Creole families in St. Louis. Kate met her French Creole husband while visiting New Orleans when she was eighteen. Two years later they married and lived in New Orleans where he was a cotton factor. When his business failed, they moved to the Cane River region of Natchitoches Parish where he became a store-keeper and manager of several small plantations. It was here that she observed the Acadians she was to write about.

Chopin is, of course, best known for her novel, *The Awakening*, but she is also the author of two collections of stories in which Acadians appear. Chopin seems to look upon this group of disadvantaged whites rather condescendingly as simple folk, basically children, innocent and natural, in need of guidance and sympathy. The men are lazy, given to fishing and dancing, and it is up to their women to prod them into the work ethic.

Several of the stories in her first collection, *Bayou Folk* (1894), involve strong daughters prodding their lazy fathers into taking responsibility for their families. In one such story, "A Very Fine Fiddle," the father can think of nothing to do when his children are hungry but to play his fiddle, "perhaps . . . to drown their cries, or their hunger, or his conscience, or all three." The little girl Fifine is finally so angered by his irresponsibility that she threatens to break his fiddle, but instead takes it to the big plantation where the owner exchanges it for one "twice as beautiful" plus a roll of money, "enough to top the old cabin with new shingles, to put shoes on their little bare feet and food into their hungry mouths." When she returns home, her father plays the new instrument, decides "it's one fine fiddle," but, apparently now ashamed of his neglect, asks Fifine to put it away, vowing that he will never play it again (98).

In another story, "A Rude Awakening," the father goes fishing instead of driving his cotton to the river landing. The daughter, angered, does the job herself, and is thrown from the wagon, rescued, and hospitalized. The story ends as the father is soundly scolded by the nearby plantation owner for his neglect.

"At the 'Cadian Ball" treats another theme of Chopin's: the relationship between wealthy Creoles and Acadians in which the caste system is always maintained with the Acadians kept firmly below the Creoles in the social structure. In this story, the childlike Acadian Bobinot vies with a Creole planter for the love of Calixta, a Cuban-Acadian beauty. The planter, however, is only courting Calixta because he has been spurned by a Creole girl. When the Creole girl changes her mind and returns to him, he leaves Calixta, who, now rejected, agrees to marry Bobinot. But she refuses to kiss him—at least "not today."

Chopin follows these characters into a later story, "The Storm," in which Calixta has now married Bobinot and borne a son. One day, during a storm, when Bobinot and the little boy are away, the wealthy planter reappears, seeking shelter from the storm. He comforts her by assuring her that her husband and son will be all right, and they end up making love. The story ends with the plantation owner gone and Calixta greeting her good-natured husband and son as they return home.

This story is interesting, particularly given the period in which it was written, for no one seems the worse for the adultery. The rich plantation owner gets to return home with no one the wiser, and Calixta, who has adjusted to her less-than-exciting marriage, nonetheless gets a brief fling with the handsome planter. And Bobinot, the "childlike" Acadian, remains happy in his ignorance. But it is important to note that the social structure is left intact. Wealthy Creole remains married to wealthy Creole and poor Acadian remains married to poor Acadian.

In a similar story, "In Sabine," a wealthy Creole planter, on his way to Texas, stops by a cabin inhabited by an Acadian girl he had known before, but who has now been reduced to a life of abuse from her Anglo-Saxon "poor white" sharecropper husband, Bud, who in stereotypical fashion, makes her work while he drinks and sleeps. During the times he is awake, he beats her, considering her even lower on the social scale than he is. The wealthy Creole is once more the hero, and one day while Bud is asleep, the hero puts her on his horse, sends her off to her parents, then climbs on Bud's horse and rides off to Texas. It is important that he does not take her with him but sends her back to her Acadian home.

In her second volume of stories, *A Night in Acadia* (1897), Chopin further develops Creole-Acadian relationships, creating in several stories a bond between a wealthy Creole benefactor and an Acadian child who is saved from a life of sloth and irresponsibility by being adopted by the Creole.

One such story, "Polydore," is typical. A Creole woman adopts Polydore, whose mother begs her to save her boy from his father's "slothful" ways. The boy, we are told, has a "round, simple face" and is "the stupidist boy to be found from the mouth of Cane river plumb to Natchitoches" (127). Not only is he simple-minded and lazy, but he is mischievous as well, playing sick often to avoid work. One day the woman is forced to go into town on an errand Polydore was supposed to do and, in the process, becomes ill and almost dies. When Polydore is overcome with shame and asks her forgiveness, she takes him into her arms, feeling like a mother for the first time, and we are given to believe that, rescued from Acadian life, the boy will become industrious and productive.

"Mamouch" again treats the theme of a prosperous Creole, a bachelor this time, befriending a poor Acadian boy, Mamouch. One day the boy mischievously lifts the doctor's gate and lets the neighbor's chickens and cattle into his garden to trample the flowers and vegetables. When confronted, he breaks down and cries. At that point, the doctor forgives and adopts him, vowing to teach him "to learn how to work; to learn how to study; to grow up to be an honorable man" (267).

"Dead Man's Shoes" offers us yet another adoption of an Acadian boy, Gilma, by a Creole planter. When the old planter dies, his poverty-stricken relatives come from Caddo and settle themselves into the house, forcing Gilma, now nineteen, to leave. They won't even allow him to take the horse the old man had given him. Gilma goes to town to see the lawyer about getting the horse—he has conceded the house—and is told the old man has actually willed the plantation to him. The boy feels immediate elation, but after thinking about the destitute relatives, one a cripple, the other a widow with two children, he decides to give them the plantation so long as he can ride off on his horse, an act revealing that he is both kind and nonmaterialistic.

One of Chopin's more poignant stories that illustrate class differences is "At Chemiere Caminada" in which a  clumsy Acadian fisherman, with eyes "almost too honest," falls in love from afar with a wealthy young woman with "blue eyes and nut-brown hair" who is visiting the Gulf from New Orleans. On the occasions when he hires out himself and his boat to take her and her friends sailing, he falls in love. One such trip, she is alone, and although he cannot understand English, she talks to him anyway. He falls deeper and deeper in love, but, of course, the class differences cause her to see him as simply lower class. When he learns that she has suddenly died, he initially grieves, but is finally relieved and happy, realizing that only in death can they be together, that class and "station," as the priest has told him, do not count with God. "There is no difference up there," he says. "There she will know who loved her best" (336).

At first "Azelie" seems only one more story of a lazy Acadian father and his intelligent and industrious daughter. It is important, however, in that it sheds new light on Chopin's view of Acadian women. Azelie is sent to the plantation store by her father to get "a li'le piece of meat," which the storekeeper gives her, and whiskey and tobacco, which he does not. As a consequence, she proceeds to steal the items. Caught in the act, she is defiant. The storekeeper, an Acadian himself, falls in love and thereafter gives her what she wants; in turn, she allows him to caress and kiss her, coming more often and asking for "luxuries" without shame. She is, we are told, "devoid of a moral sense" (230-33, 243).

If this lacking were only Azelie's, it would not hold any significance beyond this one story. The fact is, however, that Chopin's Acadian female characters always act on a practical, and often manipulative, level, but never a moral one. This might explain Chopin's refusal to make a judgment on Calixta's adultery in "The Storm." Instead of her being a more "modern" thinker than her contemporaries, which we might at first believe, it may well be that she wishes us to view Calixta's actions as not subject to condemnation because Calixta, like the other Acadians, male and female, exists on a childlike, even animal level where questions of morality are not only inappropriate but completely irrelevant. The moral sense in all of her stories belongs to the wealthy Creoles.

In all of these stories, Acadian men are lazy, childlike, simple-minded, and given to avoiding work, while the young women—we see few older women—are beautiful, intelligent, crafty, impatient with Acadian men and ready to go off with wealthy Creoles. The young boys are mischievous and will turn out as lazy as their fathers if they aren't rescued from their culture to learn from wealthy Creoles. The planters are all kindhearted and benevolent. Finally, the Anglo-Saxon "poor white" is lazy, drunken, and brutish. All of this would seem to be stereotyping on a grand scale.

Chopin is, of course, sympathetic to her characters, with the exception of the Anglo who seems to have stepped out of a story by Longstreet or Hooper. She conveys, for example, a real affection for the Acadian men, but it is an affection born of condescension. It is, in fact, that paternalism the planter class frequently exhibited toward the "children" on their plantations.

# 9

## Ellen Glasgow:
## The Dispossessed as Raw Talent

Ellen Glasgow was an advocate of progress and a modern South where reality would tear away fantasy and science would bring economic benefits to the lives of impoverished people. At the same time, her ties to the romance of the Old South were strong, and therein lies the major conflict in her novels. She was never to quite work out a satisfactory compromise.

The dichotomy seems to have been set up at birth. From her mother, whom she describes as "a perfect flower of the Tidewater in Virginia," she inherited a gentility and noblesse oblige, and from her father, "a descendant of Scottish Calvinists," a hard-headed perseverance she came to call the "vein of iron" (*The Woman Within* 139). Thus one part of her looked back on a lost civilization idealized into "heroic legend," the other looked forward to a New South where scientific farming could revolutionize and revitalize a region impoverished by long misuse, a devastating war, and the economic decline that followed.

Because of this, she seems the quintessential southerner, seeking valiantly to hold onto the old while embracing the new, never fully acknowledging that a belief in one might well preclude a belief in the other. "I had grown up in the yet lingering fragrance of the Old South, she writes in *A Certain Measure,* and I loved its imperishable charm, even when I revolted from its stranglehold on the intellect." She adds:

In the Old South, this inherited culture possessed grace and beauty and the inspiration of gaiety. Yet it was shallow-rooted; for all its charm and goodwill, the way of living depended, not upon its own creative strength, but upon the enforced servitude of an alien race. In the coming industrial conquest, the aristocratic traditions could survive only as an archaic memorial. It was condemned to stand alone because it had been forsaken by time. (12-13)

And yet a great part of Glasgow's writing seeks to preserve those very traditions in a changing world. How, she asks again and again, does one retain the "grace and beauty" of the old system at the same time one rejects that system? Her solution is Jeffersonian: hold to aristocratic ideals but seek to impart those ideals, not only to the nobility, which was fast disappearing anyway, but to the middle and lower classes as well, in order to establish a natural rather than a class-based aristocracy. To Glasgow, the process had already begun. The Civil War had been a catalyst. "Here in the rank and file," she reasoned, "men who considered themselves aristocrats marched on a level with men who did not care whether or not they were plebeians. Superficial gradations were submerged in a universal emotion" (21-22).

This is, of course, an idealization. Nonetheless, it aided Glasgow in her search for an accommodation to the new world. Perhaps the chivalric code and a sense of gentility could be preserved in a democracy. Perhaps the old caste structure was not an essential ingredient after all. Such thoughts gave her hope, at least.

But Glasgow did not base her hope on industrialization, which was the panacea for the New South advocates. Rather she looked toward a revitalized agrarian society. The problem as she saw it was that the old system had not been indigenous to the South. It had, in fact, been borrowed from Europe and, never having gained sufficient footing in this country, had gradually dissipated. In the Old South, "Southern culture had strained too far from its roots in the earth."

To recapture those roots, Glasgow maintained that southerners could no longer look to the old aristocracy, which was no longer a force, but rather to the struggling "underprivileged" farmers who, emerging from the hills to fight in the war, were staying around to demand a larger voice in the newfound democratic system. These people, not the aristocracy, were responsible for maintaining roots and thus they were the force to be reckoned with. For this reason Glasgow set out to capture in her fiction "the warmth of humble lives that have been lived near the earth" (60, 30).

In order to prepare herself for this task, Glasgow ventured out to walk beside a tenant farmer while he plowed, moving with him "up and down through the long furrows." As a result; she writes, she was able to create scenes in her novels that allow readers to feel that they themselves have been "drenched with the smell of tobacco" (32).

Therein lies Glasgow's chief stylistic success—the vivid painting of landscapes. Unfortunately, this subordination of characters to countryside seems to have prevented her from developing full-dimensional characters. This capacity, which we tend to demand of great writers, can be seen as preordained to defeat by Glasgow's proposed edict "to construct a scene in which the human figures would appear as natural projections of the landscape." Further, "all the impressions of the scene should be as primitive as the mind and heart of my leading figure, which were controlled by violence, and by the elemental motives of desire and revenge" expressed in "light and dark contrasts." These sharp contrasts, she believed, were what differentiated the country-dweller from the more sophisticated city folk whose characterizations needed to be expanded to include "more gradations" (32).

Here Glasgow may be making the mistake of assuming that the inability to express complex emotions means the person does not have complex emotions, an assumption William Gilmore Simms had made earlier about his lower-class characters (see chapter 3).

Nonetheless, Glasgow was seeking basic truths about the society in which she lived, and to do this she had to ask questions about the assumed inherent and/or inherited qualities in the individual, which justified the old system, and environment-induced qualifies, which would justify a democracy. She writes, "My own theory had inclined to the belief that environment more than inheritance determines character. What it does not determine is the tendency of native impulse nurtured by tradition and legend, unless tradition and legend may be considered a part of environment" (34). A northern writer might have been able to readily accept environment as the determining cause in this instance, but Glasgow, as a descendent of southern aristocracy, could not—at least not so easily. She must put the theory to a test. This, by her own account, she did in the early novel *Deliverance* (1904).

In that novel, Glasgow tells us, she sought to determine whether those elements commonly associated with "poor whites" are inherent. "In Fletcher, the upstart, I have treated the darkest side of transition" when society was "in convulsion" during the postwar years. His type, she asserts, was all too common in those days. Yet, is he "simply what used to be called 'a bad lot'? Or was he the victim of prolonged social injustice and the functional derangement of civilization?" She answers her own question with the reasoning that, since the type still exists in her own more liberal times, "his sins" must be "rooted in the oldest and deepest instincts in human nature, cruelty and greed." What could have rescued him from these were more genteel traditions, which he, of course, did not have (*A Certain Measure* 37).

With her characterization of Fletcher's daughter, Glasgow set herself another task—to determine whether anyone can ever truly escape the lower class. However, Maria Fletcher did not prove a satisfactory subject since she is, after all, "the higher offspring of a lower form," having "inherited a better strain from her mother" who was not of "poor white" stock. "This single strain," Glasgow concludes, "may have helped to defeat the centripetal forces of long inbreeding." Thus she had not as yet gotten to the truth of the matter, and this particular novel, she tells us, was unsuccessful. This reasoning, of course, reflects Glasgow's fascination with the theories of Darwin, especially *The Origin of Species*, which she says was "the benign and powerful inspiration" behind her first novels (38, 58).

In *The Voice of the People* (1900) Glasgow felt she was more successful in that she was able to create as her protagonist "one of the despised and rejected of society, an illegitimate offspring of the peasant or 'poor white' class" and to explore the possibility of a "civilized offspring" emerging from "primitive stock" (9, 48).

In this novel Glasgow portrays an honest man who rises to a position of power, but who retains a definite tie to the land. His undoing is his uncontrolled anger, which Glasgow sees as a lower-class trait that he hasn't been able to overcome. This anger, however, allows him to do an act of heroism which no aristocrat could have done.

Nicholas Burr, the main character, is the son of Amos Burr, a "lean, overworked man with knotted hands the colour of the soil he tilled and an innately honest face" (5). But while Amos is steadfastly tied to the life of the farmer, his son, Nicholas, is determined to break away.

Judge Battle, who loans Nicholas books to read and offers encouragement, nonetheless advises Nick to "stick to the soil." This seems to echo Glasgow's own ambivalence in that, while the lower classes are justifiably destined to merge into the middle class and assume responsibilities once belonging to the aristocracy, they are best advised to stay where they are, for in the process of upward mobility they are bound to lose their natural affinity with the land, as had the aristocracy before them. They are also likely to encounter tragedy, as does Nick when, in an act of heroism and Christ-like altruism, he sacrifices his own life to save the life of a lynch-mob victim. Judge Battle's early advice becomes, in this sense, foreshadowing of his death.

Glasgow's mixed feelings toward the emerging New South are evident also in her characterization of Uncle Ish, Judge Battle's African-American servant, who laments the passing of the Old South where everyone, including slaves and "poor whites" were comfortable because each knew his or her "place" in the class structure. Such is not the case now, he tells Nick, especially since the Judge's wife, who represented Old South values, has died:

Dar ain' no manners dese days. . . . De niggers, dey is gwine plumb outer dey heads, en de po' white trash dey's gwine plum outer dey places. . . . Dar ain' nobody lef' to keep 'em ter dey places, no mo'. . . . In Ole Miss' time der wa'nt no traipsin' roun' er niggers en entermixin' up er de quality en de trash. Ole Miss, she des' point out der places en dey stay dar. (28-29)

Nick does not heed the old man's advice, however, nor his father's objections to his getting "more schoolin" (35). He obtains an education with great sacrifice, rising early to plow the fields before going to the Judge's house for lessons. He is determined to "not be like his father . . . who was always working with nothing to show for it." He persists even over the Judge's admonition: "So you won't be a farmer, eh? And you won't stay in your class? Well, come in and we'll see what we can make of you" (43). Nick is not even deterred by his feelings of shame at having to face the other students with his coarse clothes, nor by being called "common" by the Judge's little daughter, Eugenia.

He is fortunate, however, in that the Judge overcomes his own objections to Nick's going to school, as well as the objections of the other townspeople, one of whom advises the Judge that "it is folly to educate a person above his station." To this the judge replies, "Men make their own station, Madam." Nick is also fortunate in his Sunday school teacher who ignores her father's advice that she "recognize the existence of class." Even Eugenia comes around, telling him, "I don't mind about your being poor white trash." The Judge perhaps best sums up Glasgow's theme when he says of Nick, "He has a brain and he has ambition. Think what it is to be born in a lower class and to have a mind above it" (118, 107, 119).

But there is pain involved in rising from one class to another, much of it stemming from a developing hatred for the ones left behind. At nineteen, Nick meets a farmer on the road and wonders "if he could be really of one flesh and blood with these people. What had he in common with his own father, hard-working, heavy-handed Amos Burr? No, he was not one of them and he never had been." At one point he decides that he has "never hated anyone so much as he hated his father," denouncing him as "slow-witted" and "weak." He views his whole family with hatred, in fact, now that he realizes he has become part of a "better class" (126, 97).

Nick vacillates in this, however, and after taking a job at the store to earn a living, he returns briefly to work in the fields, exulting in "the glorification of toil—of honest work well done." He resigns himself at this point to "a simple life in his own class among his own people" where he can "grow to be respected by those who were above him, finding security in their acceptance of him" (152, 160).

His determination to remain a farmer does not last long, however, and he resumes his studies, earning a law degree at the university, and going on to serve in the general assembly and as governor, becoming known as "Honest Nick" in an obvious parallel to Lincoln.

But in all of this, Nick is not able to overcome a propensity to "senseless rage" which Glasgow sees as a mark of the lower class. This is his tragic flaw, and when he intercedes to rescue the African-American from the lynch mob, it is his uncontrolled anger that defeats him. Seemingly in control of his emotions when he approaches the mob, he becomes insanely enraged when a member of the mob shouts, "Get the nigger." At that point Nick's "old savage instinct blazed within him—the instinct to do battle to death." He is killed by the mob before he can save the black (441).

And yet Nick is the only figure in the novel capable of an act of heroism. Only a person from the lower class, Glasgow is saying, has the "savage" energy to be a "hero" in the post-Civil War South. Such a man, however, is too much for society to reckon with. "It is perhaps better that he died just now," a friend tells Eugenia. "He would have tried to lift us too high, and we should have fallen back. He was a hero, and the public can't always keep to the heroic level" (443).

Therein lies the paradox that is at the heart of Glasgow's vision of the South in transition. The old aristocracy has long since been rendered ineffectual, thus the role of leadership has passed to a generation rising from the lower classes. Yet this new generation is not sufficiently rational or genteel enough to assume leadership. Without them, however, there are no leaders. It is not a particularly hopeful vision.

The novel is not as effective as it might be because of Glasgow's tendency to summarize rather than create scenes, especially when she tells us in abstract terms of Nick's frustrations, his hatred of his father, and his shame before the other, more prosperous students. These are all authentic responses to being poor, but they are presented as a sociologist might present them, and hurriedly at that. We never really feel Nick's anguish, anger, or shame. The novel is therefore significant for what Glasgow attempted rather than for what she accomplished.

Glasgow has written of her novel *Barren Ground* (1925) that it is the one she "might select . . . for the double-edge blessing of mortality" due to the principal character, Dorinda Oakley, who achieves universality because she has learned to "live without joy." Tying this theme to her own life and seemingly identifying with her character to a greater extent, Glasgow wrote that the novel "became for me, while I was working upon it, almost a vehicle of liberation" (v-vi). As such it has been seen by most critics as a feminist statement, and it is that. But equally important to Dorinda's liberation as a woman is her liberation from a past that is tied—through her father—to the futility and despair of a poverty existence.

Dorinda is perhaps the most fully realized of those Glasgow characters with a dual heritage. Her mother is from "a good family," industrious and diligent, and she brings to the marriage an ample inheritance. Her father, a "poor white," hard-working but ineffectual, proceeds "after the manner of his class," to lose the entire inheritance. He is a "dumb plodding creature" who, "like the horses was always patient and willing to do whatever was required of him," a victim of a "destiny" that has pursued him "from the hour of his birth." He is like the other "poor whites" in the valley who are dogged by destiny to an existence in which they "plod from one bad harvest to another," never dreaming anything else is possible (32, 7, 25).

A marriage such as this is a "union of the positive and the negative virtues" that produces children, each of whom inherits the virtues either of the father or of the mother. Dorinda's brother Joshua, for example, is slow-witted like his father, even acquiring "depressing" table manners, which his well-bred mother despairs of ever correcting: "There were times when it seemed to her that the gulf between the dominant Scotch-Irish stock of the valley and the mongrel breed of 'poor white' which produced Joshua was as wide as the abyss between alien nations" (36).

Rufus, the younger son, is the opposite of Joshua. He is intelligent, handsome, and "the idol of his mother" who dotes on him to such a degree that he is possessed of a "temperamental wildness" and selfishness that gets him into constant trouble. Dorinda, too, seems to have stemmed from the mother's side of the family, which accounts for her intelligence, dissatisfaction with her lot, and ultimate ability to break away from her father's sense of futility.

It is to Dorinda and Rufus that the mother turns her attention when she despairs of ever teaching her husband or her firstborn any semblance of gentility. The two youngest, she feels, "with secret satisfaction," have "sprung from the finer strain of the Abernathys; it was as if they had inherited from her that rarer intellectual medium in which her forbears had attained their spiritual being" (36).

And yet what gives Dorinda her sense of independence and allows her to escape the futility of her father's life is her realization that she has inherited good traits from her father as well as her mother. For despite his limitations, he has maintained throughout his life a closeness to nature that has allowed him to endure. This "kinship with the land" has been passed along to Dorinda "through her blood into her brain; and she knew that this transfigured instinct was blended of pity, memory, and passion." This, combined with the determination to overcome and rise above obstacles, a trait inherited from her mother, allows her to find her life's work in successful farming (233-36).

Her brothers, however, do not succeed, for they, unlike Dorinda, do not combine traits of both parents. Rufus has inherited the freer sensibility from his mother and becomes a wastrel, while Joshua has inherited the "poor white" sensibility of his father and dissolves into futility. Dorinda asks the question Glasgow had set out to answer years before: "Was it a matter of circumstances, after all, not of heredity" (233). Glasgow, one senses, would like it to be the former, but the evidence she produces points to the latter.

The problem is further compounded by Glasgow's penchant for presenting disadvantaged whites as perfectly contented to remain in their desperate poverty. This is evidenced in a minor character named Altoira Pryde, a niece of Dorinda's father, who is portrayed in the most stereotypical fashion:

All the virtues and vices of the "poor white" had come to flower in her. Married at fifteen to a member of a family known as "the low-down Prydes," she had been perfectly contented with her lot in a two-room log cabin and with her husband, a common labourer, having a taste for whiskey and a disinclination for work, who was looked upon by his neighbors as "not all there." As the mother of children so numerous that their father could not be trusted to remember their names, she still welcomed the yearly addition to her family with the moral serenity of a rabbit. (72)

Thus Glasgow's ambivalence remains to the end. And yet it does not qualify as indecisiveness or vacillation, but rather as the product of a dilemma any thinking person of her background would have faced at the time. For, as Louis Auchincloss points out, Glasgow "felt all the glorified sensations of a southern belle," even as she worked as a volunteer for the City Mission in the Richmond slums and became a Fabian Socialist (6).

Moreover, she could identify with disadvantaged whites because she saw them as suffering the same fate in the Old South as had the slave and "the woman who had forgotten her modesty." Each of these "negligible minorities," she writes in *A Certain Measure*, "may have felt inclined to protest," but they had been ignored by the writer of the time who was "satisfied with his fortunate lot, as well as with the less enviable lot of others" (135-36).

Thus she took it upon herself to record "the changing order and the struggle of an emerging middle class. . . . The old agrarian system was passing; the new industrial system was but beginning to spring up from chaos. . . . To advance or retreat, these were the only alternatives." One part of her mind wished to retreat into the "disastrous illusion" of the Confederacy, another to advance into an uncertain future (60-61, 25).

But what, after all, had the New South to show for itself when its chief preoccupation was to become "more American than the whole of America" and to replace individuality with uniformity (60-61, 25, 27)? One could not look to the newly powerful industrialist for inspiration, for he, like the banker in *Virginia* (1913), was more apt to be sitting in his office, looking out over the town to his factory, ignoring the vast pockets of poverty that existed in between (83).

If one thus saw the old aristocrats as impotent and the industrialists as insensitive, where was one then to find hope? Obviously in the emerging middle-class, especially the as-yet-untried "poor whites" who were making their first strides at gaining political and commercial leverage. "Before the war one hardly ever heard of that class," says a character in *The Miller of the Old Church* (1911). "It was so humble and unpresuming—but in the last twenty-five or thirty years it has overrun everything and most of the land about here has passed into its possession" (84).

But what can one make of a class that over the years has been forced to become as "lean and depleted" as the soil they till (*A Certain Measure* 158)? Obviously, one cannot look to the already destroyed older generation but must look instead to a new generation that has not been through long years of being defeated by the circumstances of an older system. But these young people must come from only a certain type of poor family, the "good people" who own their own land, not the "poor white trash" who do not (*Barren Ground* 4-5).

But even here one's hopes are dashed, for the newly emerging class is fast becoming corrupted by the capitalist system they are seeking to democratize. As one of the older generation of aristocrats says in *The Miller of the Old Church*, "These people have learned a lot in the last few years, and they are learning most of all [that] the accumulation of wealth is the real secret of dominance" (100-01). Of that novel, Glasgow has written:

I have portrayed the better type of the plain countryman who forged ahead, after the social upheaval, and became a power in the confident dawn of Southern democracy, before that new fiber of that democracy had weakened under the combined weight of ignorance and self-interest. . . . Will the declining strain of the aristocracy be enriched or depleted by the mingling of the social orders? Will the fresh infusion of blood save the old way of living? Or will it merely hasten the end of an incurable malady? (*A Certain Measure* 128)

Glasgow was never able to answer the question.

# 10

## Elizabeth Madox Roberts:
## The Dispossessed as Human Being

Unlike Ellen Glasgow, Elizabeth Madox Roberts felt no compulsion to lament the passing of the southern aristocracy, perhaps because her Kentucky ancestors were far removed from the gentry of tidewater Virginia. Her father descended from a man who had emigrated from Virginia to Kentucky in the late eighteenth century, and her mother from a bond-slave who had come to America in 1750. Roberts was thus not inclined, as had been Glasgow, to elevate her lower-class characters into inheritors of the aristocratic tradition. And in her stylistic movement inward through the stream-of-consciousness technique, she revealed a belief in lower-class sensibility and sensitivity that far surpassed Glasgow's.

Roberts's understanding of how it feels to be poor may have come partly through her own experience as one of eight children in a family that was living, as Robert Penn Warren puts it in his introduction to her *The Time of Man*, "in the backwash of war, in what would euphemistically be called reduced circumstances but was, in brutal fact, poverty" (viii). It cannot be said, however, that Roberts knew the experience of the generational "poor white" tenant farmers she writes about in her famous novel. For her father, who served under Bragg in the Confederate Army, was a farmer, schoolteacher, civil engineer, and merchant, and he imparted to her knowledge garnered from books that would not have been available to the daughter of a sharecropper.

But Roberts did feel alienation as a child, which would lead to an understanding of that part of the experience of being poor. For she remembers as a child "sitting on the dark stairs . . . alone, shaking with misery . . . [feeling] akin to no one" (qtd. in McDowell 23). Added to this was her experience as a young schoolteacher in Springfield, Kentucky, where she encountered on an intimate level, the lives of the dispossessed poor, and experienced the frustration of trying to give a sense of self-worth and the importance of education to children programmed to fail.

There can be little doubt that she would have felt what countless other rural schoolteachers have felt—and indeed are still feeling—the agony of not being able to penetrate the awful barriers that poverty has for generations set up in the minds of otherwise intelligent and capable children.

This frustration could well have been part of the driving force that caused her to quit teaching after ten years and to return to school, this time at the University of Chicago where she met writers who were her entree into the literary world, which in turn allowed her to return to Kentucky and begin, at age forty, to write the novel that would bring her international fame, *The Time of Man* (1926). It was in this novel that she set down her feelings about poverty and, in the process, created perhaps the most sensitive and intelligent portrait of disadvantaged whites in the annals of American literature.

As that novel opens, Ellen Chesser, the daughter of a tenant farmer, is fourteen years old, living in a "poor trash house," and dreaming of a home "with vines and trees and flowerpots" and "a room to sleep in" (12, 56). She also dreams of wearing "a blue hat with a big white ostrich plume . . . and white slippers on my feet" (54).

But Ellen is constantly reminded that she is poor, seeing even street vendors as better off than she is: "Many of the people must be richer than herself, she thought, for they had things to sell in baskets and things in brickets—eggs, butter, sorghum molasses . . . a few of them, she supposed, must be very rich, those riding high stepping horses or driving in high traps" (59). Like many another poor child, Ellen seeks some elevation of status by mentally separating herself from those people she calls "trash," while at the same time she is made by others to feel that she cannot escape that label herself. The landlord's wife, for example, makes her feel as though she has lice crawling on her. Lice, to Ellen, are a manifestation of "trashiness" and thus a constant threat (39, 145).

There are other threats, of course, other constant reminders of her poverty. She recalls, for example, having to beg for clothes, and when she is traveling on the road with her family, she watches prosperous people as they pass by, but if they look at her she suffers "great shame" (48, 40). She finally asks herself, "Why am I here and what is it all for anyway" (97)?

Ellen finds her answer as an adult in a simple resolution to continue to live, to endure. Hens continue to brood, she reflects, even though rats eat the young as soon as they are out of the nest (145). This sentiment, a reflection on life pushing forward in the face of adversity, gives her strength to endure a great deal of hardship, including a failed romance, an adulterous husband, and the death of a child. At the end of the novel we see her on the road with her husband and remaining children, seeking "some better country, some fertile, well-watered land," although she appears to have few prospects. In fact, the only sign that anyone of her family will escape poverty is in her young son's longing to read books. The reader, however, remembers all too well that Ellen as a child had also wanted to read books, but this had not served as a passage from her subsistence way of life.

Roberts made known that her purpose in *The Time of Man* was to create an "Odyssey of Man as a wanderer buffeted about by the fates and the weathers" (qtd. in McDowell 37). And this she has done in an extremely poetic style. But therein lies a problem—reader accessibility. For in her constant attention to Ellen's innermost thoughts and reactions to events, she loses the sense of narrative necessary to convey those events to the reader. According to John M. Bradbury, Roberts is "rather a student of poetry than of the art of the novel [and] seldom achieves the unity of tone or the proportion which a complete work of fiction requires" (45).

Her fault does not lie, however, as James Mallard would have it, in unsuccessfully trying to transplant "a soul out of Virginia Woolf . . . into a simple tenant farm girl" (352). Such criticism not only seeks to lessen Robert's achievement, but insults the poor in general. For while there is every reason to know that uneducated farm girls are incapable of expressing themselves in sophisticated language, there is every reason to believe that tenant farm girls, like other people, have complex human emotional responses to the events of their lives, despite their lack of an adequate vocabulary with which to relate those responses to others. In fact, it is this entrapment in self, so well portrayed by Roberts in both content and style, that is the tragedy of the poor of all races. Perhaps it is the ultimate tragedy of humanity itself.

# Part Three:

# Reinforcing the Stereotype

# 11

# The Persistence of the Stereotype

Condemning the poor has long been a practice in the nation as a whole, but it has been an especially prevalent one in the South. Sociologists Michael Morris and John B. Williamson offer this reason.

In a stratified social system . . . power and communication primarily flow downward. There is little opportunity for middle-class persons to be confronted with data challenging their projections about the psychology of the poor, much less to be confronted with poor people who can indicate how institutionalized blockages are preventing them from fulfilling their positive orientations. (447)

Add to this poor people's propensity to see themselves in the same way society sees them and we can recognize the enormity of the problem. Peter H. Rossi and Zahava D. Blum tell us that, since the tone in our society is "decidedly middle-class . . . by implication, the lower-status individual finds himself negatively evaluated" and, in fact, receives "poorer treatment at the hands of schools, stores, banks, law-enforcement agencies, medical personnel and landlords" (50).

Morris and Williamson emphasize the treatment in schools that children of poverty receive as central to their development of low self-esteem, citing a number of studies that confirm that "the teachers' stereotyped expectations and behaviors with respect to these pupils contribute to a self-fulfilling prophecy taking place in the school setting" where a "lack of verbal interaction and encouragement" lead to poor academic performance and withdrawal, "thus confirming the teachers' initial low expectations. Moreover, internalization by these children of negative stereotypes concerning their academic potential is likely to increase the probability of such a self-fulfilling prophecy occurring" (451). Clearly, writes Lola M. Irelan, "economic deprivation is a fundamental limitation which permeates all of life" (vi).

And yet the stereotype persists. Even an essentially sympathetic writer like W.J. Cash could, in his *Mind of the South* (1940), describe disadvantaged whites as having "no power of analysis" and say of southern millworkers who joined unions that they did so not out of class-consciousness, for that would have taken a "complexity of mind" they did not possess, but rather "as a novelty," as part of their "simple childlike psychology." They were, he said, "willing to join any new thing in sight, from a passing circus to the Holy Rollers." And, in words that further echo the prevailing stereotype of African-Americans, he suggests that "tin-horn fraternal orders" flourished in milltowns because they "afford [the millworker] an opportunity to strut in uniform or costume" (166, 249).

But the twentieth-century writers who most pointedly defend stereotypical attitudes toward disadvantaged whites are the Agrarians of *I'll Take My Stand* (1930). Reacting to what they felt had been a takeover of the South by reformers and advocates of "progress" —including capitalists, liberals, socialists, communists, and sociologists—they used the caste system of the Old South as a metaphor for the kind of society the present day South should have.

John Crowe Ransom, in the opening essay of the volume, does not claim that the Old South was a perfect society, only that it was the most perfect America has produced. Real perfection had only been achieved in Europe, particularly in England where civilization had been achieved centuries before and humanity had long since made peace with their environment and established a "stable economic system" in which they could relax and enjoy cultural pursuits (7).

The Old South had a system very close to this, according to Ransom. For having established "a sufficient economic base" dependent on slavery, which Ransom maintains was "more often than not, humane in practice," southerners, unfettered by ideas of progress and material gain, pursued "the life of the spirit." They could not match "the finish of the English," however, because they had too recently emerged from pioneering days and society hadn't settled enough into a completely established order before the Civil War broke out. In particular, the differing social classes had not had time to become "fixed" as they were in England; rather they were "loosely graduated," a situation in which "it could not be said that people were for the most part in their right places" (13-14).

However, according to Ransom, a stable society where people would know and keep their place was on the verge of becoming a reality in the Old South. Southerners were primed for it. They had passed the pioneering stage and were ready to move into the fully civilized one. But then came the "invasion from the North," bringing with it "liberalism" in the guise of "service," planting discontent among the lower classes, black and white, convincing them they were not as happy as they thought they were (10-11).

John Gould Fletcher begins his essay "Education, Past and Present," by seeking to exclude "poor whites" from the educational system because of their innate inability to learn. The purpose of education, he argues, "is to bring out something that is already potentially existent in the human being," and since it is obvious there is no potential in rural children, seeking to educate them beyond elementary school is a futile endeavor. "If we are nothing to begin with," he writes, "no amount of education can do us any good" (93).

Reformers, he maintains, have long misinterpreted Jefferson, who never called for educating the poor. Instead he had merely "asked that the poor but brilliant pupil should have an equal opportunity with the well-to-do but lazy one." All other poor children should be satisfied with an elementary education. The people of the South agreed with Jefferson, according to Fletcher, which is why the practice came about whereby the rich planters sent their sons to the academies, while the poor sent theirs to "pauper schools," which prevailed until the time of the Civil War (104-11).

After the war, Fletcher continues, a defeated and bankrupt South, seeing that its old academies could not be revived, bowed to federal critics and set up a system of public schools where everyone, rich and poor, was to be given an education. This was a mistake, for trying to educate the poor, or for that matter, any child from the country, was a complete waste of time. What good is it, he asks, to send the farm child to school only to have him or her return to the farm to plow and wash dishes? He sees as equally absurd educating African-Americans, arguing that though the high school and college courses are so simple even "the negro" can pass them, "it is a waste of money and effort to send him there," considering that he is destined to work at menial tasks not requiring education (115-19).

Whom then, Fletcher asks, should we educate? His answer: "the superior"—those modern equivalents of the "gentlemen" of the Old South who are capable of achieving "character, personality, gentlemanliness in order to make our lives an art and to bring our souls into relation with the whole scheme of things, which is the divine nature" (120).

Clearly such high aspirations are not for the African-American or the rural white, or for that matter, women. These groups, he says, constitute "the inferior" who should "exist only for the sake of the superior." And yet, our public school system has turned everything upside down, putting "that which is superior—learning, intelligence, scholarship—at the disposal of the inferior" (121).

Lyle Lanier's "Critique of the Philosophy of Progress" in the same volume is essentially an argument that industrialism by necessity harnesses "uniqueness" which can only flourish in an agrarian society. It is only in such a society that "superior, dominant individuals" can emerge to articulate "the impulse of a people" (144-47).

The most interesting aspect of Lanier's essay, however, is his solution for unemployment. Simply put it was this: "The large surplus of chronically unemployed should be induced by all possible means to return to agriculture." Lanier doesn't explain how millions of unemployed could be absorbed in a system that had already driven large numbers to the city for employment, and which was currently starving millions.

Andrew Lytle, in his essay "The Hind Tit," argues that dissatisfaction with unbridled capitalism and industrialism would lead modern people to find escape in "the three final stages industrialism must take"—socialism, communism, and sovietism—the latter invading the sanctity of "the yeoman South" by collectivizing agriculture itself, the last bastion of "free men" (203, 208). The greatest danger in this, as far as Lytle is concerned, is that the ruling class is destroyed in the process: "Those who accumulate great estates deserve whatever reward attends them, for they have striven mightily. This is the common way a ruling class establishes itself. The South, and particularly the plain people, has never recovered from the embarrassment it suffered when this class was destroyed before the cultural lines became hard and fast" (209-10).

This is what happened during the Civil War, according to Lytle, which is why the "plain people" became discontented, a situation that hadn't existed under the old order. For then, these people had lived happily in the hills, their days filled with "pleasant conversation, the excitement of hunting, fishing, [and] hearing the hounds run." After the war, however, they came down from their idyllic life to acquire land left vacant when the aristocracy was wiped out. But, unlike the aristocracy who had ruled "naturally," these "plain people" were fast enslaved by their indebtedness to the merchants and to the tenant system itself, which drew social lines not according to natural superiority of character as in the Old South but rather according to how much cash one had. Thus did the formerly independent, free-minded "yeoman" become "the poor white, the hookwormed illiterate" (212-15).

Robert Penn Warren, in his essay "The Briar Patch," sees "poor whites," along with blacks, as victims of the slavery system. "The fates of the 'poor white' and the negro" are "linked in a single tether. The well-being and adjustment of one depends on that of the other." Since both compete in the manual labor market, Warren offers Booker T. Washington's solution for both: vocational education.

What happens, however, when they are trained? There will then be competition for the same jobs, a competition Warren asserts the African-American is "better equipped to win" because he is willing to accept wages the white "could not possibly live on." The white, in frustration, resorts to "violence, sabotage, and persecution" (259).

To such a scenario there would appear to be no happy outcome. Yet Warren offers one: cooperation for the benefit of both races. The "poor white" can learn, "either by expensive and bitter experiences or by an exercise of simple intelligence that color has nothing to do with the true laying of a brick and that the comfort of all involved in the process depends on his recognition of the fact" (26).

Warren seems the most humane and democratic of the Agrarians, but in the end, he is condescending to both the "poor white" and the African-American in that they, unlike himself, should avoid the city life and a formal education. Nonetheless, his views were too liberal for the arch-Agrarian Donald Davidson, who questioned Warren's right to be included in the book.

Stark Young, in his essay "Not in Memoriam, But in Defense," restates the Agrarian case for "superior blood." The ideal behavior of the slave-owning planters, he maintains, provided the basis for manners and mores for all southerners, "even in this day." Such qualities derive from the maintenance of pure blood lines. "Our tradition of family involves the fact that so many of our families come from the British Isles . . . and remained unmixed with other bloods." Thus "the notion in general of kin and family . . . the source of so much proud and tender emotion . . . goes back to one of the oldest racial instincts." A man's love of kin, both for his ancestors and those yet unborn, stems from the fact that "his blood runs in [their] veins," creating a sense of honor and pride handed down from generation to generation (347-48).

Young relegates the "poor white," who in reality came from the same stock as did the landed gentry, to a position lower than segregated blacks. They are simply "more shiftless" and "less self respecting" than their neighbors and for this reason deserve the fate of never being "invited farther than the front steps" of a self-respecting citizen's home (352).

Such sentiments were not shared by all southerners at the time, of course. Nonetheless, the Agrarians did set the tone for the acceptance of literature that would treat disadvantaged and dispossessed whites in much the same way that Byrd, Simms, and the Southwest humorists had treated them. Thus did the "redneck" stereotype reemerge in the critically sanctioned literature of the southern renaissance superseding the more humane characterizations of Harris, Cable, Glasgow, and Roberts.

# 12

# William Faulkner:
# The Dispossessed as Tragic Hero
# and Comic Villain

Given the serious and sympathetic treatment of disadvantaged whites by a long line of post-Civil War writers from Joel Chandler Harris to Elizabeth Madox Roberts, Faulkner's depictions of the Snopes clan seem a regression to the antebellum attitudes of William Gilmore Simms and the Southwest humorists, who saw such people as grotesque threats to the established order. In the antebellum world, such attitudes were both conservative and defensive because of the the realistically perceived threat from the North felt by the planters and their allies. But by Faulkner's day, such attitudes could be construed as reactionary.

However, Faulkner emerged as a writer at a time when many southerners had realized that the progress promised by advocates of a New South had not come to pass, that instead the South had acquired industrialization without prosperity, becoming, in their eyes, simply a poverty-striken replica of the North.

The solution, it seemed to many, including the Agrarians, was to recall the "best" of the antebellum system and seek to preserve it. This meant holding to the old caste system where everyone knew his or her place and where, as John Gould Fletcher put it, the "inferior" existed "for the sake of the superior."

Important outward signs of "superiority" had always been land ownership and control of government. When these areas appeared to have been invaded by "inferior" people such as the Snopeses—who were initially landless tenant farmers—the result, according to the displaced aristocracy and their defenders, was the death of gentility, taste, and traditional values. In short, the caste system, which they felt had embodied the best that man had thus far devised, had evolved into a democracy that represented the worst.

Speaking to a literature class at the University of Virginia in 1957, Faulkner said of the Snopes clan: "I have hated them and laughed at them and been afraid of them for thirty years now" (Gwynn and Blotner 201). In this statement, we can easily see the Snopes saga as Faulkner's dramatization of the still-lingering antebellum nightmare that saw Jacksonian democracy as ultimately producing chaos.

Robert Penn Warren, however, set the tone for much of contemporary Faulkner criticism when he wrote that the Snopes clan were not Faulkner's representative "poor whites" at all. Those Warren saw as more accurately the Bundrens in *As I Lay Dying* (1930). The Snopeses, he maintained, were not so much to be taken for "poor whites" as representatives of mechanized man in modern society. To illustrate Faulkner's fondness for the Bundrens, Warren rightly points to the poetic language used to record the thoughts of the individual family members. The writing there, he says, "is charged with sympathy and poetry" *(Selected Essays* 73).

It is true that there is much eloquence and poetry in the thought of the Bundrens, and it would seem that this is Faulkner's honest attempt to reflect complexity of thought and emotion that he must have believed "poor whites" were capable of. Consider, for example, Darl's use of such words as "suffused," "surreptitious," and "soporific" (64, 67, 69). Clearly, Faulkner did not believe that an uneducated person would actually know these words. Nonetheless, he has Darl make full use of them in his soliloquies.

The reason seems obvious. Had Faulkner limited himself to words Darl and the other Bundrens would have actually used, the reader would have taken the simple words to reflect simple thoughts and emotions. This is the trap many a realistic writer has fallen into—trying to express the deepest, most complex thoughts of their characters in the words those characters would actually know. By elevating the language of the Bundrens, Faulkner has shown us that inarticulate people are as capable of emotional complexity as their more educated counterparts, even though they don't always have the words to outwardly express what they genuinely feel. Darl, of course, is the most intuitive of the Bundrens.

Warren is on less firm ground when he cites Addie's poetic thoughts, for, after all, Addie is not really "poor white" at all in origin. She was a middle-class schoolteacher who, to escape that life, marries a "poor white" and lives to regret it, feeling apart from both her husband and their children. Jewel, to whom she is partial, is a product of her illicit relations with a minister who is also not lower class.

There does seem to be a serious attempt on Faulkner's part to convey the reality of poverty, but this is often overshadowed by episodes reminiscent of the Southwest humorists, such as those involving Dewey Dell as the stereotypically ignorant hill girl, naive and voluptuous, who is taken in by the drugstore clerk's seduction on the absurd premise that a second act of fornication will get rid of the baby conceived in the first act.

This propensity is also evident in Faulkner's treatment of Anse Bundren. The comic device most prominently used here is Anse's obsession with getting a new set of teeth, but Faulkner also uses repetition and incongruity—reasoning that at first glance appears absurd, but upon closer examination actually has some sense to it. For example, Anse constantly complains that he is "a luckless man" and blames his troubles on the fact that a road has been constructed close to his home. The latter conclusion loses its illogicality, however, when we recall Andrew Nelson Lytle's fear, expressed in *I'll Take My Stand*, that "good roads" throughout the South were signaling the end of the agrarian system (236).

Nonetheless, there is evidence that Faulkner sees Anse as in some sense tragic. If we are to believe Darl, and there is no reason not to, Anse, who is seen as incurably lazy and dependent on others at the time of the action of the novel, was not always so. In fact, as a young man he had been a hard worker who fell deathly ill "from working in the hot sun," a reality that gives credence to his otherwise superstitious belief that if he works up a sweat he will die.

Darl also sees that behind Anse's "slack-faced astonishment, he muses as though from beyond time, upon the ultimate outrage." Darl also relates that Anse's feet are "badly splayed, his toes cramped and bent and warped . . . from working so hard in the wet . . . homemade shoes when he was a boy." And Tull describes Anse as "dignified, his face tragic and composed" when the neighbors come to view Addie's corpse, but this, of course, might be more a mask than anything else, given Anse's bent for acting (49, 7).

In this novel, however, Faulkner moves from high sentiment to low humor, from elaborately poetic and elevated language to broad slapstick. Witness, for example, Addie's rotting corpse, the smell of which bothers everyone who comes close, except for the Bundrens themselves, who don't seem to notice. These scenes seem inspired by George Washington Harris's depiction of Sut Lovingood burying the decomposing body of the widow Yardley, as does Vardaman's drilling holes in Addie's skull.

And the ending in which Anse parades down the street with his "duck-shaped" wife in tow, along with a record player and a new set of teeth, could well have been written by Erskine Caldwell. In this final episode, we are jarred out of a sense of tragedy as the elevated language of earlier passages gives way to rustic humor. In the process, whatever dignity Faulkner attributed to his characters in the earlier chapters dissipates.

In *Absalom, Absalom!* (1936), however, the issue of class distinctions has tragic, not comic, implications. The action of the novel revolves around Thomas Sutpen, who, as a young boy, moves with his family of "poor whites" from the mountains of West Virginia to tidewater country and encounters class prejudice for the first time when he is told that he must go to the back entrance of a plantation house. It is this single representative incident that sparks Sutpen's motivation and sets him on a course of action that destroys the lives of so many people, including his own, as he decides, in Faulkner's words, "to take revenge for all the redneck people against the aristocrat who told him to go around to the back door" (Gwynn and Blotner 97).

It is significant that when Sutpen gains a position of power akin to that of the planter who had snubbed him, he acts in a similar fashion toward the granddaughter of the "poor white" Wash Jones. It is also significant that Jones, a replica of an earlier Sutpen, is shocked from an admiration of Sutpen in the same way that Sutpen, as a boy, had been shocked from his admiration for the Virginia planter. Wash also takes revenge, killing Sutpen and his granddaughter, then moves toward a group of men he knows will kill him. Thus does the tragedy come full cycle.

In an attempt to answer a student's question as to why Sutpen desired "respectability," Faulkner replied:

He wanted more than that. He wanted revenge as he saw it, but also he wanted to establish the fact that man is immortal, that man, if he is a man, cannot be inferior to another man through artificial standards or circumstances. . . . [He] was trying to say in his blundering way that, why should a man be better than me because he's richer than me, that if I had had the chance I might be just as good as he thinks he is, so I'll make myself as good as he thinks he is by getting the same outward trappings which he has, which was a big house and servants in it. He didn't say I'm going to be braver or more compassionate or more honest than he—he just said, I'm going to be as rich as he was, as big as he was on the outside. (qtd. in Gwynn and Blotner 35)

It is obvious that Sutpen, who is so humiliated by the rebuff at the plantation house that he hides in the woods for a time, does not conceive of changing the caste system. In fact, there was nothing in his life or the life around him to indicate the possibility. Instead he took the understandable position of deciding to join the system, but in the process realized that the only way to gain respect in such a system was to acquire what his oppressors had, and the only way to do this was to not worry about compassion or honesty. In losing these qualities, however, he loses his humanity and brings about his own destruction.

Sutpen tries, of course, to gain a measure of respectability through marrying into a "good" family, but he is unsuccessful, for the "respectable" people reject him as soon as he arrives in town "with a horse and two pistols and a name which nobody heard before." He is simply not a "gentleman," according to Miss Coldfield, and "marrying Ellen or marrying ten thousand Ellens could not have made him one" (14-16, 52).

Sadly enough, Sutpen does have a past, and he retreats into it when he is snubbed by the majority of the townspeople, staging fights between his "wild" slaves, even wrestling with them himself and inviting as audience people Miss Coldfield refers to as "riffraff who could not have approached the house itself under any circumstances, not even from the rear." In addition, he engages in long conversations with Wash Jones, which leads Wash into admiring him so much that he equates him with "God himself." For this reason, Wash is intensely hurt and angered when Sutpen gets Wash's granddaughter pregnant and then, when she is about to give birth, cruelly remarks, "Well, Milly; too bad you're not a mare too. Then I could give you a decent stall in the stable" (28, 282, 286).

Melvin Backman sees Sutpen's tragedy as stemming from his denial of his own background, from giving up "the values of the frontier for those of the property-caste system." Faulkner's sympathies, he writes," seemed to be on the side of the backwoodsman," whose life may well be more crude and brutal than the planters, but at the same time is "more honest and natural and innocent, simply because it was not founded on and sustained by property, by slavery." In the process of carrying out his design to build a dynasty, Sutpen "had lost a family; in making himself into the image of the southern planter he had lost part of his humanity; in displacing conscience by pride, he had lost the power to see into himself" (99, 107).

Cratis D. Williams makes a similar statement. Sutpen's "basic trouble," he writes, "was the destruction of his innocence." Emerging from the hills and encountering injustice against his class, Sutpen takes "revenge on the social order that had so dramatically relieved him of his innocence" (353). Myra Jehlen elaborates on Sutpen's loss of innocence, adding that this takes place when he realizes "the perversity of social ethics by which only those who did nothing useful were considered human while he and his family lived and indeed were become like brutish cattle inhabiting rotten log cabins." This reaction, according to Jehlen, was typical of many such objections to the caste system at a time when there was growing fear among some southerners "that excessive power over other human beings and over-abundant leisure might undermine the character of the southern gentleman" and when "the majority of whites in the region enjoyed very little leisure and looked askance at their social betters" (61-63).

Faulkner himself seems to have a certain admiration for, and sympathy with, Sutpen, who is, as Backman notes, "the only heroic figure in the story." Moreover, Sutpen combines elements of both planter and "redneck" as both had been envisioned by earlier writers. In actuality, of course, the planter was closer to Sutpen than those writers wanted to believe. Backman demonstrates this by pointing out that "with the possible exception of Sartoris, all the founders of the ruling class in Yoknapatawpha [County] . . . got their land by hook or by crook," and that even Sartoris is pictured in The Unvanquished as possessing a "violent and ruthless dictatorialness and will to dominate" (256-58). Jehlen adds: "Sutpen as lord and peasant both can embody the entire South corrupted and ultimately destroyed by the plantation system. . . . Indeed, with Sutpen as a focus, the more torn Faulkner feels between the conflicting loyalties to planters and rednecks, and the more he empathizes with the former while voicing the complaints of the latter" (65).

As biographers have pointed out, there is a great deal in Faulkner's family background to create in him both an affinity for, and fascination with, Sutpen. Faulkner's paternal great-grandfather was fond of telling the story of how he, at the age of fifteen, migrated from Missouri to Memphis "on foot . . . a poor, sick, ragged, barefoot, penniless boy." He married into money, like Flem Snopes, and became extremely wealthy through business ventures, including the building of a railroad, exploiting others along the way. In the end he was shot to death by a business partner. He embodied, according to Frederick R. Karl, "a frontier energy" manifest in a "ruthlessness in exploiting others, an expedience in his dealings with human life, and an apparent indifference to consequences." He also, in Snopes fashion, sold contraband goods during the last years of the Civil War—after engaging in various skirmishes with his briefly organized Partisan Rangers—and later entered politics as an advocate of the "poor man." Thus, Karl concludes, Faulkner's family ties were to both the aristocratic Sartorises and the "poor white" Snopeses, although "the Snopes aspect . . . may not have been one" that Faulkner "cherished" (35-48).

All of this pulling together of the southern experience allowed Faulkner to create in Sutpen a character with truly tragic dimensions. But in the Snopes trilogy that follows, Faulkner abandons high tragedy for low comedy, and Thomas Sutpen dissolves into Flem Snopes. Both are "poor whites" who come out of the hills possessing "no past" as far as the "respectable" citizens can ascertain, and both formulate a design by which to gain wealth and power by whatever means available. But whereas Sutpen comes to a tragic end for doing so, Flem is rewarded by success.

The major trouble with Faulkner's Snopes theme is that it is historically false. While it is true that the old aristocrats did lose power, it was not at the hands of "poor white trash." Jehlen, echoing numerous scholars, writes that impoverished whites, "on the farm and off," did not rise in any significant numbers, but rather "moved about the southern economy horizontally," not vertically, giving Faulkner "little historical justification" for his portrayal of the rise of the "redneck" (140).

Nor is there justification for Faulkner's repetition of the old theme of inherent blood differences between the "better" families and the "trash." Indeed, as historians have noted, both emanate from the same stock. Yet, when Ab Snopes in "Barn Burning" destroys other people's property, or in the words of the narrator, displays a "voracious prodigality with materials not his own," this practice stems not so much from any individually derived motivation as from the fact that he has it "in his blood." Barn burning, we are told, is an inherent trait.

Sarty also feels the "old fierce pull of blood," and obeys his father out of "old habit, the old blood which he had not been permitted to choose for himself, which had been bequeathed him willy nilly and which had run so long (and who knows where, battering on what of outrage and savagery and lust) before it came to him."

It is significant that while all the Snopses are driven by this old pull of "blood," Sarty, who breaks the blood tie and runs away, is dropped by Faulkner after this story and does not appear in the Snopes trilogy at all. It is also significant that the "good" Snopes, Eke, who is honest and hard working and displays the characteristics of pity and compassion that the Snopes family as a whole lack, is described as having a father who was not a Snopes.

There is an ambivalence, however, when Faulkner introduces the character V.K. Ratliff in *The Hamlet* (1940), for Ratliff, unlike the omniscient narrator of "Barn Burning," exhibits a kind of bemused tolerance of the Snopeses, attributing to Ab motivation beyond "blood" by saying at one point, "He ain't naturally mean. He's just soured" (27). At another point Faulkner has Ratliff say of Lump Snopes, "I am stronger than him. Not righter. Not any better, maybe, but just stronger" (198).

Rafliff, however, is a sewing machine salesman and therefore far less threatened by encroaching "rednecks" than are the aristocracy. Moreover, Faulkner counters Ratliff's tolerance with the views of the aristocratic Gavin Stevens and his nephew Charles Mallison. Gavin's alarm, in fact, seems closer to Faulkner's own words to the University of Virginia students: "I feel sorry for the Compsons. That was blood which was good and brave once, but has thinned and faded all the way out. Of the Snopeses, I'm terrified." for they "can cope with the new industrial age," while the Compsons can only endure in the face of the "redneck" onslaught, "not by organizing or combining forces, for that would achieve nothing, but by registering individual protest" (qtd. in Gwynn and Blotner 197, 80).

It might be more accurate to say, however, that Faulkner's attitude is actually a combination of the views of Ratliff and Stevens. For he gives to the more tolerant Ratliff the earlier Snopes episodes before the Snopeses become a real threat to society as a whole. When they move beyond Frenchman's Bend and threaten to overpower Jefferson and the surrounding area, their actions are interpreted for us by less tolerant Gavin Stevens and his nephew.

It is apparent, however, that while Faulkner saw a need to temper Steven's alarm with Ratliff's bemusement, he clearly intends to leave us with Gavin's interpretations. Even the tolerant Ratliff is, in the end, driven to agree with Stevens when the latter, going off to war, asks, "Think you can hold them [the Snopeses] till I get back?" and Ratliff replies, in a remark we can take as humorous but which almost seems a softened version of Kurt's solution to the African "savages" in "The Heart of Darkness." "The only thing," Ratliff says, "is to get shut of them, abolish them" (*The Town* 33).

Clearly, in a world where the traditional values of honor, justice, and honesty—tied to the aristocracy and land ownership—are constantly threatened with extinction, there is little hope, particularly if the only remaining defenders of the old order are people such as the ineffective Gavin Stevens. Surely such a man cannot hold back the advance of the Snopeses, who represent the worst aspects of industrialism and entrepreneurship—those forces that have invaded and transformed an agrarian south into a mechanized and moral nightmare.

Warren supports his view that Faulkner is not portraying the Snopeses as representative "poor whites" by noting that they are descendants of bushwhackers who made their assault not only on the old aristocracy but on "the plain, hard-working small farmers" as well (75). It is true, of course, that Ab Snopes was a bushwhacker during the Civil War. But it is also true that Faulkner is following the tradition of distinguishing the honest "yeoman" farmers from the "poor whites" represented by the Snopeses. In Faulkner's view, as in the Agrarians' view, the "yeoman" attains his status by having always owned his land, whereas the sharecropping Snopeses have never owned land before their descent from the mountains. Thus they cannot share in the inherited values which "yeoman" farmers have in common with the aristocracy. "People of their kind," we are told in *The Mansion* (1959), "never owned even temporarily the land which they had rented between one New Year's and the next one. It was the land which owned them" (91).

Faulkner is historically accurate in his depiction of how the land was mortgaged after the war and fell into the hands of merchants like Will Varner. But that is where historical accuracy ends. For Will Varner, in turn, sells the land to the cunning Flem

Snopes, which Faulkner sees as the ultimate insult to tradition. The Snopseses, having never owned land in the old days and thus having never acquired the old values associated with the land, are not prepared ethically or otherwise to uphold traditions they aren't even aware exist. The new South—commercial, industrial, and dehumanized—has truly arrived, controlled, according to the narrator of *Light in August* (1959) by "hookworm-ridden heirs at large" who are rapidly assuming positions of financial and political control, just as the defenders of the caste system of the antebellum south had feared they would.[1]

Because the myth of the rising "poor white trash" to positions of power has been shown to be false, it is difficult to agree with George Marion O'Donnell and other critics who insist that Faulkner is "really a traditional moralist in the best sense" (82). For inherent in his system is the indictment of a group of people who, whatever their faults, are not the evil usurpers of the power structure in Mississippi or anywhere else. Such an indictment can only serve to isolate the much-maligned "redneck" further into a stereotypical object of derision and hatred.

A standard stereotype of the disadvantaged white is that he is lazy, stupid, and behaves like an animal, and Faulkner often presents him as such. Provine, in "A Bear Hunt," for example, loafs "in a brooding, saturnine fashion wherever he will be allowed" and makes "no effort whatever to support his wife and three children." The narrator further declares that "there are other men among us now whose families are in want; men who, perhaps would not work anyway."

It is interesting, however, that in *As I Lay Dying*, only Anse is characterized as lazy and we are given a rationale for his laziness. No one, moreover, is portrayed as stupid or behaving like an animal, if we except Dewey Dell, who suffers the fate of other Faulkner females. Faulkner can, in fact, be given high marks for seeing some aspects of the effects of poverty quite clearly, namely low self-esteem and shame. This is seen when Dewey Dell insists, "We are country people, not as good as town people," and when she assures Vardaman that Santa will still give him the train set even though he is not a town boy," and again when Vardaman asks Anse, "Why ain't I a town boy, Pa? . . . God made me." Finally, when Darl compares his father to Vernon Tull, he points out that he has "never seen [Tull] go to town in overalls" (38, 42, 6).

Faulkner also gives Anse a sense of pride which, however ironic, seems at least admirable. "We would be beholden to no man," he says and refuses an offer of food with, "We got a little something in the basket. We can make out." Even his persistence in keeping his promise to Addie to bury her in Jefferson is presented as an admirable trait (12, 130).

Yet when we leave the Bundrens for other lower-class characters in Faulkner, pride and motivation often disappear, and stupidity and animal imagery increase. Lena Grove, for instance, is described as "sheeplike," and although we are privy to her innermost thoughts, she never seems to think beyond inane superficialities like "I have come . . . a fur piece," which ends chapter 1 of *Light in August,* and "My, my. A body does get around," which ends that novel.

Moreover, animal-like, Lena doesn't seem to be concerned that she is about to deliver, except for the perfunctory comment that she finds it "a little difficult" to crawl out a window. And she is too limited in intelligence to make a connection between her telling Lucas Birch she is pregnant and his leaving, which, of course, links her to Dewey Dell and Eula Varner (6, 16). Boon Hogganbeck, we are told, has "the mind of a child, the heart of a horse, and . . . eyes without depth or meanness or generosity or viciousness or gentleness or anything else." In other words he is totally an animal *(Go Down Moses* 252).

But Faulkner pulls out all the stops when he describes the Snopeses. Ab is "wolflike" and his daughters "bovine" ("Barn Burning"). Flem is compared to a small hawk, I.O. to a weasel, Lump to a chipmunk, Mink's children to dogs, and Mink to a "cotton mouth." To compound the animal imagery with stupidity, Faulkner has Eke mistake "hog piss" for coal oil, Isaac gets defecated on by a cow, and Lump's mother isn't aware that "she had actually never had enough to eat" *(The Hamlet* 51, 160, 74, 91, 197).

Some Faulkner critics counter that it doesn't matter whether or not Faulkner is historically, sociologically, and psychologically accurate. O'Donnell, for example, maintains that the Sartoris-Snopes conflict is universal. It is, he says, a metaphor for the worldwide battle between good and evil (84). And there is Warren's justification of the Snopeses as symbols of modern mechanized humanity.

Faulkner, however, is on record as saying that "the writer is too busy trying to create flesh-and-blood people that will stand up and cast a shadow to be conscious of the symbolism that he may put into what he does or what people may read into it." There is symbolism to be sure, he said, but it is secondary to the creation of "people" (Gwynn and Blotner 47-48, 58, 74, 147). Faulkner realized that characters in fiction must work on both realistic and symbolic levels to be accepted by discerning readers. Moreover, it should be said that our struggles are always against particular enemies, even though, as Sam Keen notes in *Faces of the Enemy*, we tend to abstract them into "apparitions of the hostile imagination." We do this because it then becomes easier to oppose them (46-47).

Thus when Charles Mallison explains that "when I say 'we' and 'we thought' what I mean is Jefferson and what Jefferson thought," it is obvious he considers himself an insider and is excluding "white trash" from being considered Jeffersonians (*The Town* 3). Such is also the case in "Barn Burning," when Major deSpain's house, a haven of "peace and dignity," is threatened by Ab's cold and unfeeling anger. If this anger extends to an entire class, that is, if Ab becomes symbolic of the "redneck" in general, then the situation becomes truly desperate for defenders of the status quo who see their values and inherited life style threatened. Such a fear leads them to view the lower class as either invaders to be opposed or comic figures to be dismissed out of hand. Faulkner saw them as both; hence his comment that he was terrified by the Snopeses at the same time that he found them funny.

Either way, however, he is thinking in stereotypes, and his art suffers, so that from the poetry of *As I Lay Dying* and the high tragedy of *Absalom, Absalom!* he descends into the barnyard comedy of the Snopes trilogy, adding to his work three novels that significantly mar an otherwise impressive canon.

# 13

# Erskine Caldwell:
# The Dispossessed as Grotesque Victim

Erskine Caldwell is a curious figure in southern literature. Seemingly pulled in two opposing directions, he could, on the one hand, write about impoverished white tenant farmers so victimized by the sharecropper system as to cause Donald Davidson to denounce him as a "Southerner who turns state's evidence" (qtd. in Korges 16). On the other hand, he could rival Longstreet's condescending portrayals of disadvantaged whites as savage buffoons.

But whereas Longstreet's immediate appeal was to Jackson-era defenders of the old order who enjoyed seeing landless whites portrayed as subhumans unworthy of the vote, Caldwell's purpose, according to his own testimony, was to call attention to his subjects' desperate living conditions. A great deal of his vast audience, however, seems to have read him for the same reason that a wide audience read Longstreet—to laugh at stereotyped "poor white trash."

Caldwell remains a curious figure today because of what appear to be diametrically opposed fictional aims—one a truly serious commitment to social and economic reform, most probably acquired from his Presbyterian minister father, the other a penchant for grotesque comedy, more than likely inspired by readings in literature and tall tales about "crackers" and "tar heels." His statement in *Call It Experience* that he got his characters solely from observation (103) should be taken with a grain of salt. Granted, he may well have walked along the countryside depicted in *Tobacco Road*, but it is hard to imagine that he saw such behavior as a young girl copulating in her front yard as her father and other family members, as well as passersby, watch in amusement.

Just how close Caldwell is to Longstreet is readily apparent in an early story, "Savannah River Payday," from his collection *American Earth* (1931), a story that, except for the appearance of an

93

automobile, might well have been a sketch in Longstreet's *Georgia Scenes*. For in it two "rednecks," Jake and Red, tear into each other at the least provocation. In one scene, which is a bit too reminiscent of the famous fight episode in that earlier work, Red hits Jake over the head with a monkey wrench and "a ball of skin and hair [fall] in the dust." In another scene, Red slices his friend's ear off. Jake, in the manner of Longstreet's "clay eaters," is not the least bit resentful of this, despite the fact that he continues to bleed profusely throughout the story.

Caldwell's seeming confusion of purpose is compounded as the two pick up the body of an African-American who has been killed by a falling tree. They strap him to their running board to take him into town, all the while complaining of the smell from his rotting corpse. A grotesque touch is added as the dead man's lips swell in the sun so that "they curled over and touched his nose and chin." Grotesquerie and violence are compounded when Jake proceeds to knock out the dead man's gold teeth with a monkey wrench. In a further development reminiscent of Harris's *Sut Lovingood* and Faulkner's *As I Lay Dying*, Red and Jake leave the corpse strapped to their running board while they remain inside the poolroom for the better part of the afternoon.

Throughout the story the objective tone of the narrator is maintained to such a degree that we are unaware as to how we are meant to respond to the story. Had Caldwell written nothing else, we could assume that this is simply an insensitive story meant to be funny. But we know from Caldwell's other work that he did indeed have a serious message to convey about the condition of both "poor whites" and African-Americans. We might well ask in that context if this is supposed to be an indictment of the white southerner's attitude toward blacks. Sadly, there is nothing in the story to indicate that we should read it this way. In fact, the comic techniques utilized defeat such a reading.

A similar confusion of purpose is revealed in another story in the same volume entitled "Joe Cradock's Old Woman," although here the author's serious statement is evident in that it is clearly superimposed on the ending. It is, nonetheless, not fully apparent whether we are supposed laugh. Note, for example, that in an otherwise serious description of the effects of a life of poverty on a farm woman—her hair "coarse and stringy, and dingy," her face "creased into lines of toil and hideousness"—Caldwell inserts a crude reference to her breasts as having "fallen flat to her chest like saddle-flaps."

The seriousness of Caldwell's message is evident, however, when this woman, who is seen by her husband as "repugnant," dies and is prepared for burial by the undertaker, at which point, bathed and shampooed, she appears to the husband to be actually beautiful in the same way she appears in a picture taken of her when she was a young girl. The story ends as he sits beside the casket staring at his dead wife, taking in her beauty which he had not been aware of during their entire married life, overshadowed as it was by the devastating marks of an impoverished existence. The crudely "comic" touches, however, damage the seriousness of the theme.

No such problem exists in the wholly tragic story "Dorothy," where Caldwell drops the comic techniques used in other stories. If one remains—exaggeration—it creates more melodrama than comedy. The serious tone is engaged immediately when the first-person narrator is asked directions to an employment office by a starving young woman and he directs her instead to a row of cheap hotels that house prostitutes. In his moves to other cities, he is haunted by his act and finally vows to return to Atlanta and find her. The story is so grim in its details, however, that we are not convinced of the protagonist's ability to save her from a life of prostitution.

The serious strain in Caldwell manifests itself in a strong and often heavy-handed indictment of southern farming practices in *Tobacco Road* (1932), a novel that reveals Caldwell's awareness of contemporary historical and sociological studies. He gives Jeeter Lester, for example, a family history that begins with his grandfather, whose plantation had contained "the most desirable soil in the entire west-central part of Georgia" and ends with Jeeter on a small section of the original land unable to eke out a living on the depleted "sandy loam." "An intelligent employment of his land, stocks, and implements would have enabled Jeeter, and scores of others who were dependent upon Captain John to raise crops for food, crops to be sold at a profit. Cooperative and corporate farming would have saved them all" (83-86). The problem with this passage and similar ones throughout the text is that they cause the novel to shift abruptly and incongruously from fiction to political tract.

Caldwell even allows Jeeter, despite his animalistic primitiveness, to realize that he is a victim of the system and to express anger toward those in power. "You rich folks in Augusta," he says at one point, "is just bleeding us poor people to death. You don't work none, but you get all the money us farmers make" (149). Lov reiterates this theme in a summation of Caldwell's message at the end of the novel: "It looks like the Lord don't care about crops being raised no more like He use to, or he would be more helpful to the poor. He could make the rich people lend out their money, and stop holding it up. I can't figure out how they got hold of all the money in the country, anyhow. Looks like it ought to spread out among everybody" (237).

Such passages appear to stem from an honest desire to expose the sharecropper system, which was, as Caldwell indicated in a preface to a 1974 edition of the novel, "an often ignored though dominant element of the South" (vii). This theme, however, is overpowered and ultimately defeated by Caldwell's bent for depicting his subjects as animalistic idiots undeserving of the serious attention he demands for them. And while he wishes his message to be a progressive one—the overhaul of the entire economic system—the effect of his characterizations leads to a conservative conclusion—that one might as well leave these creatures where they are, for no amount of reform could ever get them to behave like human beings.

Caldwell, in fact, seldom allows the Lesters to act in a human fashion. For example, the old grandmother, who has lived so long that the family considers her "nothing more than a door-jamb or a length of weather-boarding," is shoved out of the kitchen, left to starve, and is finally run over by her grandson, after which Jeeter gazes at her lifeless body and says, "She ain't still yet, but I don't reckon she'll live. You help me tote her out in the field and dig a ditch and put her in" (225).

Thus is the family portrayed as completely lacking human feelings or intelligence—except for Pearl. She, the narrator tells us, "had far more sense than any of the Lesters." To explain this, Caldwell follows the pattern of writers from Glasgow to Faulkner, suggesting other than a "poor white" parentage for her. Her father is someone who passed through the country one day, and has not been seen since (40). Pearl, we note, will have nothing to do with her "poor white" husband, Lov.

And yet Caldwell was capable of occasionally portraying disadvantaged whites as human beings, at least to a degree. An example of this is Will Thompson in God's Little Acre (1933), a character referred to by others in the novel as a "linthead" but who emerges as a hero in the most archetypal sense, sacrificing himself for the good of the community.

Ty Ty Walden is, of course, the character who most often comes to mind when we recall the novel, and many mistakenly believe him to be a "poor white," when in fact he owns one hundred fertile acres and employs two blacks as tenants on his land. In addition, everyone in his family eats well and none lack adequate clothing, except, of course, when they shed it to engage in sexual activity. A further distancing from "poor white" status is given them by Caldwell in their speech patterns, which are, on the whole, standard English.

Ty Ty's financial situation is, in fact, far from destitute and has arisen solely because he has dug up nearly all of the farm's perfectly good soil searching for gold. To further establish him as "boss," Caldwell has him repeat the callous behavior of landowners in such stories as "Kneel to the Rising Sun" by gruffly telling his hungry tenants not to bother him by asking for rations while he has his mind set on his search (46-47).

It is Will Thompson, however, rather than Ty Ty, who dramatizes Caldwell's social message. One of a group of strikers who have been locked out of the cotton-mill because they have demanded more than the starvation wages paid by the company, Will becomes the conscience of the others, conveying to Ty Ty "how strong men were in the Valley when they were young and how weak they were when they grew up breathing cotton lint into their lungs and dying with blood on their lips. And . . . how pretty the girls were when they were young and how ugly they were when they were old and starving with pellagra" (259).

It is because Will sees this and is determined to do something about it that he becomes the spokesman for the entire community of strikers. Elevated to almost superhuman status in their eyes, he becomes a sacrifice for them when he breaks into the mill and turns on the machines and is gunned down by company guards. He provides a sharp contrast to Ty Ty's two grown sons: Buck, who is cuckolded by Will, and Jim Leslie, a wealthy real estate broker who spends his time foreclosing on tenement dwellers in the city.

In "Kneel to the Rising Sun," a story from a collection of the same name that appeared in 1935, Caldwell portrays a disadvantaged white character sympathetically, although not heroically, in Lonnie, a tenant farmer who is afraid to display his lean, hunger-ridden face before the landowner for fear of being reprimanded for reminding the landowner that he is starving his tenants. He also does not allow himself to "show any anger or resentment" for fear that "Arch would drive him off the farm before sundown that night."

Caldwell, however, doesn't give Lonnie more than primitive intelligence, and his blind obedience to authority, although it conveys the utter hopelessness of a class beaten down by centuries of discrimination, nevertheless serves to render him as only a cut above, or perhaps equal to, his dog Nancy. It is to his fellow tenant, the African-American Clem, that Caldwell gives the human, even heroic traits of courage, fortitude, and independence. And while the author's intent seems to be to show how debased one can become under longtime oppression, the characterization of Lonnie unfortunately serves to reinforce the stereotype of the "poor white."

An important difference between Lonnie and Jeeter Lester, however, is exhibited when Lonnie and Clem drag Lonnie's father away from ravaging hogs. Lonnie is genuinely saddened by his father's death, even though the old man has been a burden on his family, just as Jeeter's mother had been a burden on his.

"Daughter," which may be Caldwell's most solemn story, illustrates the extremes to which the author felt a man could be driven by frustration and despair over his inability to feed his children. The protagonist kills his daughter because she is starving to death and he can no longer stand to hear her say she is hungry. Too proud to beg, he takes the only action he feels available to him, and when he is put in jail, a crowd of men, who share his frustration and hunger, liberate him from his jail cell.

The curiousness of this story is not only in the unbelievable actions of the crowd who sympathize with a man who murders his daughter, but in Caldwell's assumption that the reader will sympathize with him also. This story, more than any other, shows Caldwell's tendency to be seduced by his message.

"Slow Death" uses first-person narration by a character close to Caldwell's own experience. It thus rings truer. A grim tale meant to reveal the destitution that existed in the early 1930s, it is set in Augusta where the narrator, standing on a bridge that spans the Savannah River, describes homeless people pitifully huddled below him, including "a family of four living in a cluster of dry-good boxes." There are a dozen or more crates on the South Carolina side, and "when old men and women, starved and yellow, died in one of them their bodies were carried down to the river and lowered into the muddy water." Caldwell's plea for action against such injustice is made through Dave, an unemployed manual laborer who tells the narrator, "As soon as the people know what to do, and how to do it, we can go up and run hell out of those fat bastards who won't give us our jobs back."

Dave, who insists that the narrator share his last fifty cents, demonstrates a communal spirit that Caldwell sees as sadly lacking in the power structure of America. But in a scene that is a shade too contrived, Dave is hit by a car, and, as he dies in the street, he is taunted by the driver, who accuses him of purposely jumping in front of his car and "faking" his injury. Although clearly adapting a defensive posture to justify his own mistake, the driver nonetheless represents the callousness with which so many Americans, according to Caldwell, regard the down-and-out.

Another illustration of the prejudice middle-class people often feel toward the less fortunate is in "Man and Woman" from the collection *Southways* (1938). In this story, a young couple, Ring and Ruth, walk down the road, hungry and desperate, begging from house to house for food. More often than not they are refused. One housewife lectures Ruth on the value of work, assuming that anyone who doesn't have a job isn't trying to find one. "I wouldn't call him much of a husband," she says, "to let you walk though the country begging food." When Ruth tries to tell her than Ring has been sick for five weeks and has lost his job because of his illness, the woman refuses to believe her, persisting in her stereotype of the poor. "Why didn't you stay where you were instead of making tramps of yourselves?" she asks. "Can't he hold a job, or don't he want to work?"

*Trouble in July* (1940) is not ostensibly about disadvantaged whites, but its protagonist, Jeff McCurtain, is one of the most maligned and stereotyped of figures—the "redneck sheriff." The difference between McCurtain and similar characters that appear all too often in movies and on television is that McCurtain, during the course of the novel, actually grows out of the stereotype.

He begins the novel in typical Caldwell fashion, concerned about the white citizens of his county only to the extent that they will vote for him. In the same manner, he is concerned about blacks only in that they should be lynched without his knowing it. Whenever he hears that a black is about to be lynched, he immediately goes out of town on a fishing trip.

Now, however, he cannot avoid a lynching that is about to occur, the reason being that the man controlling enough votes to defeat him in the next election is a landowner who fears that if the black is not lynched, "there won't be a nigger left on my plantation by sundown tomorrow night," insuring that his crop will not be harvested. McCurtain had better allow the lynching to proceed, he tells him. If not, "he'll never get another vote in this part of Julie County" (25).

A problem arises when the lynch mob enters the jail and drags out a totally uninvolved black named Sam Brinson simply because they can't locate the black they have wrongly accused of raping a white girl. McCurtain sets out to rescue Brinson although he knows he may well be sacrificing his career. When Brinson is found safe, and it is evident that the original black has been lynched, McCurtain says, "I'm thankful I saved one out of the two," a statement he seemed incapable of making at the beginning of the novel.

Caldwell does create a "poor white" stereotype in Shep Barlow, a tenant farmer and father of the girl who has supposedly been raped. He is quick-tempered, having once slit a man's throat for getting a drink from his well without asking. He also reacts to his wife falling into the same well by getting angry, tossing wood in after her, and then digging a new well. His fifteen-year-old daughter is also stereotyped as yet another of those Caldwellian "poor white" teenagers whose only goal in life is to get men to copulate with them.

*Tragic Ground* (1944) is Caldwell's account of what would have happened to Jeeter Lester and his family had they moved to the city. In this novel, the Lester family has been replaced by Spence Douthit, his wife, and their two daughters. It is wartime and the family has been recruited from their native Beaseley County to work in a powder plant in a large Gulf Coast city. For an unspecified reason, the plant is closed, leaving Spence unemployed and homeless, having been evicted from the company house. He, along with many of his fellow workers, who have been recruited in a similar fashion from across the South, find shelter in Poor Boy, a section of town largely ignored by the city, where they exist either as squatters or as dwellers in low-rent ramshackle houses.

A basic difference between Jeeter Lester and Spense Douthit is that, while Caldwell seems to have genuine affection for Jeeter —viewing him as not only a victim but someone who recognizes his animal instincts and acts upon them—he seems to have little if any affection for Spence who, unlike Jeeter, is not a "natural man." He is instead, just plain "trashy," possessing no redeeming qualities whatsoever. When he is given money by a kindhearted but naive social worker so that he can go back to Beaseley County, he proceeds to spend it on gambling and whiskey, sharing part of the latter with his neighbor's wife and hiding the rest under the porch for himself. He also becomes easily resigned to his daughter's having become a prostitute, urging her, in fact, to marry her pimp because "he makes a lot of money" (123). Moreover, in a game of musical beds, Spence wakes up beside a fifteen-year-old girl and grapples with her in what is hard to view as other than an attempted rape (229).

But whereas *Tobacco Road* was an indictment of the sharecropping system in the country, *Tragic Ground* is an indictment of the welfare system in the city, for it is the crippling influence of government handouts that is the chief villain in this novel. "There ain't no sense in doing without," Spence concludes, "when there's people who make a business of giving away money" (155).

There are, of course, sympathetic "poor whites" in the novel. Floyd Sharp, for one, kills the pimp who is in the process of having sex with his twelve-year-old daughter. Floyd afterwards turns himself into the police, telling Spence, "They'll send me away for a while, but they'll put my girls in a home and take care of them" (222). And Jim Howard, who marries Spence's older daughter, finally takes the family back to Beaseley County, delivering Caldwell's message: "The ones who own the land are to blame for not putting up better houses and the city is to blame for not doing something about it. You know yourself it's nothing but a rat hole, and people can't live like human beings very long in a rat hole" (118).

It is obviously Caldwell's intention to condemn capitalism, which creates Poor Boys, as well as the welfare system, which further entangles its recipients in poverty and corruption. The problem once more, however, is that in rendering his chief victim as totally corrupted, he reinforces the notion that such people are beyond redemption and simply "trash." Spence himself perpetuates this stereotype when he happily proclaims that, back in Beaseley County, his family was known as "the doggone Douthits," and then adds, "It seems to fit somehow" (107-08).

But if we judge from this that Caldwell has abandoned "rednecks" to negative stereotypes, we get a totally different picture in *A House in the Uplands* (1946) where he turns the tables to portray the aristocracy as "trashy" and the dispossessed whites as virtuous. In this novel, which is a further indictment of the tenant farming system, Caldwell eschews humor throughout and the result, once more, is melodrama. But the novel does seem to be a serious attempt to draw a more complete picture of his native region in order to round out what he called a "Cyclorama of Southern life."

Because it is melodramatic, however, *A House in the Uplands* is full of stereotypes, the most obvious being the chief character, the aristocratic Grady Dunbar, who having inherited five thousand acres of once rich but now depleted cotton and timber land, proceeds to let it all go to waste, mortgaging it to the hilt so that he can drink and gamble. He is totally insensitive to his black tenants, whom he keeps in virtual bondage by manipulating the account books so that they end up owing him more money for rations than they have earned in wages, thus guaranteeing their remaining on his land. He also exercises complete control over his white overseer, Will Harrison, and his family, whom he persists in calling "low-whites."

Grady finally gets his comeuppance when his wife becomes aware that he is sleeping with a quadroon in one of the cabins, and he learns his lesson, summing up his own situation at the end of the novel a little too neatly with the cliché-ridden observation that "I'm one of the down-and-out aristocracy. We've petered out. Everybody knows that" (199).

Will Harrison closely parallels the white tenant farmer of "Kneel to the Rising Sun" in his subservience to his boss. Caldwell reveals this in an effective, if obvious, use of irony, when Will cautions an old black not to cross "Mr. Grady" because "you know yourself that a colored man can't afford to disobey a white man. . . . This here's a white man's country." A short while later, he unwittingly qualifies that statement to show that it is actually only a *rich* white man's country. "I've always tried to do everything Grady tells me to do," he says," and one of those things is not stepping out of my place" (102, 114).

It is left to Will's wife to summarize Caldwell's position on the class system when she tells her husband, "He [Grady] treats us the same way he does the colored up there in the quarter—like dirt. . . . God in heaven never gave any man the right to lord it over human beings the way he does us" (95).

A more positive future for the South is manifest in two characters. One is Ben Baxter, an ex-profligate aristocrat who has since worked his way through law school and whose practice involves promoting justice for both blacks and impoverished whites, calling for an end to the "peonage" system. The other is Will Harrison's son, Brad, who is resolved to fight the system also and accuses his father of perpetuating the status quo by approaching Grady with "your tail between your legs." Moreover, he openly defies Grady, despite the latter's threat that he knows "how to teach you low-whites a lesson to make you stay in your place" (123).

Thus Caldwell agrees with Faulkner that the aristocracy is doomed, but unlike Faulkner, he does not lament their demise. In fact, he welcomes it. And in making the middle-class Ben and the lower-class Brad spokesmen for a New South, he is more in line with Glasgow, whose character Nicholas Burr in *The Voice of the People* is a clear progenitor for both.

Caldwell does not give a totally positive spin to the novel, however, for he has the newly freed wife of Grady Dunbar choose between Brad and Ben Baxter. Her choice is clear and unhesitating; it is the one who comes from a "good" family. It is Brad, however, who has the last word and thus presents Caldwell's final statement on the rapidly changing social system. After being rejected as a suitor, he shouts at her in defiance: "I'm not good enough for you, am I? . . . You won't have anything to do with me because I'm low-white! I should've known it! You're just like all the rest of them. . . . Go on and stay with your kind, but one of these days you'll wish you'd taken up with me when you had the chance" (238). Because these are the closing words of the novel, they appear to be Caldwell's prophecy, or perhaps hope, of an emerging, newly resilient lower-class white.

If *A House in the Uplands* represents an advance in Caldwell's social philosophy, however, *This Very Earth* (1948) signals a setback. Chism, a rural type transferred to the city, is Spence Douthit revisited, but even more debased than Spence. He too has been thoroughly seduced by the welfare system. His one ambition in life, he says, has always been to move to the city because, unlike farmers, "they take life easy, same as I want to do. When they don't feel like working, they just set and rest, and if they don't have enough to eat, the city comes along and hands out some money to buy groceries with" (14).

Also like Spence, Chism is perfectly willing to let his daughter, who works as a waitress, support the family while he engages in his own pursuits, which include introducing his eleven-year-old son to whiskey and to "high yellows" whom he entraps and forces to undress for his son's benefit. But unlike Spence, whose transference was not of his own making, and who was willing to work, at least for a while, Chism sells his farm to buy a shack in town and thereafter makes no pretense about job-seeking.

Nor does his live-in son-in-law, who spends his time playing snooker for side bets at the pool hall while he is not abusing his wife, Dorise. To Dorise's request that he go to work so they can have a house of their own, he responds, "You're crazy. . . . Every thing's free here. It doesn't cost a dime to stay here. Why should I break my back at a job just so I can pay house rent and buy groceries. I'm staying right here. I know when I'm well off" (34-35).

Grandpa gives us the philosophy behind the events. "We'd never have come to this if we'd stayed on the homeplace," he says. Maybe Chism's two boys will get back to the land, he thinks. It is, after all, a generation thing. He elaborates on this theme: "It looks like God is set and determined to show us how imperfect we are by seeing to it that a good family skips a generation of its kind every once in a while and produces a generation of black sheep instead. The finer and stronger a family gets, the more it's likely to happen" (137).

Is this what Caldwell has come to, a simple explanation of social conditions that reduce his characters to being a product of fate rather than injustice, insuring that they cannot therefore be altered by reforms he had advocated earlier? An educated guess might be that he had, by the late 1940s, grown weary and disillusioned, for, after all, there was no longer the Depression to explain the impoverished condition of disadvantaged whites, although many areas of the South did not share in the general prosperity of the nation as a whole. Or one might surmise that an author who was willing to display his "poor white" characters in the most unfavorable light possible, and whose primary predilection seems to have been toward condescending comedy in the vein of the Southwest humorists, might well have been swayed by reformist ideas so prevalent in the 1930s, but retreated from those ideas later in life.

Sylvia Jenkins Cook in her book *Erskine Caldwell: The Fiction of Poverty, the Flesh, and the Spirit* offers what is perhaps the most acceptable explanation for Caldwell's negative portraits of his subjects when she writes:

Caldwell utterly rejected the notion that poor people must be virtuous in order to deserve relief from their poverty, and equally the reformer's notion that such relief would make decent citizens out of wily rogues.

His residual Presbyterian vision of human nature saw all mortals as undeserving and irrational, yet only the poor and vulnerable were forced to add further material deprivation to their innate depravity. (284)

Cook argues at another point that Caldwell "portrayed individuals as variously irrational, foolish, and vicious, but he attacked fiercely a social system that exposed them to hunger, disease, and persecution" (5).

If this is true, and Cook has shown that it probably is, then Caldwell's purpose was sorely undermined by his method which, as Louis D. Rubin has noted, is squarely in the Southwest humorist tradition of "looking down at the rustic primitive from above, with mingled amusement and astonishment." Rubin makes the further observation that "if we grant an underlying seriousness of literary purpose [to Caldwell] . . . then it was betrayed by a vision of caste and class that has been characteristic of southern literature almost from the beginning" (*Gallery* 169).

Caldwell has denied, of course, that he was ever motivated by a desire to reform society. To an interviewer he revealed that "once in a while I get the feeling that people think I'm trying to reform something or trying to change something. All I'm trying to do is make a story interesting to myself." This response comes into question, however, when he proclaims in the same interview that his favorite nonfiction book of all that he had written was *You Have Seen Their Faces*, a book whose call for reform is hard to miss. More to the point may be Caldwell's statement that "comedy and tragedy go hand in hand in my opinion. Everything in life is susceptible to one or the other, and there is no difference in my mind between them. . . . What could be a funny joke at one point would be a very sorrowful event at another. It might be the same happening" (Collins 40, 43, 261).

This observation goes a long way to explain the seeming contradictions in Caldwell's writings. It also reveals a tragicomic sense that is not evident in the writings of most American authors and is more akin to European writers like the Irish playwright Sean O'Casey.

There is a basic difference between Caldwell and O'Casey, however, even though both took as their subjects "poor white" characters and elicited laughs at their expense. O'Casey knew, as Caldwell did not, the truth of Fielding's adage that the true source of humor is affectation. This is readily apparent in *Juno and the Paycock* when Captain Boyle pretends to have sailed around the world as captain of a ship. It is also apparent in his pretense to learning in his continual misuse of intellectual terms, in his pretense to poetry in his declaration to the stars, and in his pretense to philosophy in his statement that "the world's in a terrible state of chassis."

One cannot imagine O'Casey treating in comic fashion starving people grappling over a few turnips or an old woman treated by her family as if she were a piece of weatherboard. Nor can O'Casey be accused of looking down his nose at his characters. This may be explained by the fact that he experienced in childhood the extreme poverty he gave to his characters, while Caldwell did not.

# 14

# Flannery O'Connor:
# The Dispossessed as Redeemer

Flannery O'Connor cannot be said to be overly fond of her lower-class characters, but then neither is she overly fond of her characters from the middle class. In fact, she seems quite democratic for, as Claire Kahane says, "she directs her acidic wit at all her characters" (184). If one measures the acidity, however, it seems more aimed at middle-class women like Mrs. Hopewell and the Grandmother in "The Misfit" than at her characters of the lower class who, more often than not, function as catalysts to knowledge and messengers of truth as O'Connor sees it.

Stanley Edgar Hyman's observation that O'Connor is depicting "Georgia Snopesism" (30) is not really true, however, even though, as Mrs. Turpin says in "Revelation," the social order has been turned upside down with "the bottom rail on top" and the "respectable" citizens at the mercy of their "inferiors." It is also true that the poor endure in O'Connor in the same way that the Snopses endure in Faulkner.

But unlike the Snopeses, O'Connor's dispossessed whites often bear witness to the "truth" of the corruption of the world and point out to their more prosperous counterparts the need for redemption. And when middle-class characters like the Grandmother in "The Misfit" or Mrs. May in "Greenleaf" are jolted into seeing this truth, it is a lower-class character who does the jolting, often through violent means. What usually occurs is that the middle-class characters are initially smug in their feelings of superiority to the lower class only to discover that they have been taken advantage of by someone they consider inferior and, in the process, have become displaced in the social order. This realization, however, leads finally to their "redemption." Mr. Shiftlet of "The Life You Save May Be Your Own" is one example of O'Connor's "redneck" conveyers of truth. Bearing a name of stereotypical "poor white" connotations and a body so disfigured

that it seems to form "a crooked cross," making him an obvious
Christ figure, Shiftlet tells the old woman, "Nothing is like it used
to be, lady. . . . The world is almost rotten."

Later, Shiftlet is seized by a revelation and, realizing that "the
rottenness of the world was about to engulf him," he prays for
rain to "break forth and wash the slime from this earth!" At this
point, the heavens open, rain begins to fall, and Shiflet steps on
the gas in a burst of energy and races "the galloping shower into
Mobile."

In "A Circle of Fire," O'Connor contrasts two women, one a
middle-class landowner with the ironic name, Mrs. Cope, who is
"continually being astonished" by life, the other, her opposite, a
realistic and sardonic "poor white," Mrs. Pritchard, who is obviously secure in her being. Mrs. Cope reveals her innocent smugness and sense of false superiority when she prides herself "on
the way she handled the type of mind that Mrs. Pritchard had."
At the same time, however, Mrs. Pritchard is viewing Mrs. Cope
"with contempt."

Mrs. Cope, similar in temperament and outlook to other
middle-class characters in O'Connor, takes pride in owning "the
best kept place in the county" which she has maintained, according to her own testimony, by hard work and keeping an eye on
her "irresponsible" employees. As is the case of the old woman in
"The Life You Save May Be Your Own," however, Mrs. Cope's
well-regulated life is intruded upon by outsiders—three lower-
class boys, one the son of a former employee. These boys proceed
to destroy her complacency by acting in an insolent manner,
riding the horses she has asked them not to ride, and finally setting fire to the woods they claim do not belong to her but to God.

In the last scene, Mrs. Cope, shocked at last out of her smugness, hears "shrieks of joy" from the boys she now equates with
"prophets . . . dancing in the fiery furnace, in the circle the angel
had cleared for them." In her awakening, she takes on a "new
misery," an awareness about life that makes her feel at one with
all those she has hitherto felt superior to. Thus truth for O'Connor involves an awareness that social lines are artificially drawn
and those who feel socially superior need a lesson on their true
status.

Naive feelings of false superiority are revealed also in "The
Displaced Person" in the characterization of Mrs. Mcintyre, a
landowner who feels she is at the mercy of "poor white trash and
niggers" who keep leaving her employment simply because they

are "that kind of people" who "don't want to work." "I've had enough trashy people on this place to last me a lifetime," she says, assuming that her employees, white or black, should show gratitude for her having hired them in the first place. In the end, the hired hand, Mr. Shortley, goes off "to look for a new position" and the African-American employee leaves in order to satisfy "a sudden desire to see more of the world"—both departing in what we are given to feel are not unhappy circumstances for them, while Mrs. Mcintyre, faced with declining health, waits out the remaining years of her life with her only visitor being an old priest who sits by her bed and explains Church doctrine although she can no longer hear him.

Mrs. Hopewell in "Good Country People" is another smug middle-class character who feels she has had "plenty of experience with trash" and is thus able to differentiate "trash" from "good country people." Her capacity for judgment, however, is blatantly exposed when she readily accepts the corrupt Bible salesman. Even her cynical daughter is deceived.

The only characters in the story who "see" in any realistic sense—given O'Connor's view of the world—are the "common" characters, Mrs. Freeman, who is fascinated by "hidden deformities," and the Bible salesman, who tells Mrs. Hopewell that despite her protestations to the contrary, "People like you don't like to fool with country people like me" and then proceeds to humble Mrs. Hopewell's overly haughty and arrogantly "intellectual" daughter, Joy, reducing her to absurd helplessness by taking away her artificial leg.

Mrs. Hopewell's false assumption that she can determine "good country people" from "trash" prevails to the end, however, when, still ignorant of what has happened to her daughter, she remarks to Mrs. Freeman that the Bible salesman is "simple." "The world would be better off," she says, "if we were all that simple."

Another such landowner, in "Greenleaf," is Mrs. May, who has "put up with" her tenant family, the Greenleafs, for fifteen years, feeling they have "no worries, no responsibilities," living "like lilies of the field, off the fat that she struggled to put into the land." Paralleling Faulkner's aristocratic and middle-class characters' fear of the rise of the Snopeses, she proclaims that in twenty years the Greenleafs will be "Society" and her efforts to make a go of her farm will be for naught. Her fears, in fact, seem to be borne out when she is killed by a bull belonging to the Greenleaf boys, and in her last earthly moments, she appears to be whispering "some last discovery into the animal's ear."

"Revelation" is the story of yet another land-owning female protagonist, Mrs. Turpin, who is forced to share a doctor's waiting room with members of differing social classes, including a "white-trashy" family whom Mrs. Turpin sees as "worse than niggers any day," thanking the Lord that she was born neither "poor white trash" nor "nigger." Moreover, like Mrs. May and Mrs. Hopewell she feels she knows "trash" sufficiently well to make all sorts of rash judgments for "there was nothing you could tell her about people like them that she didn't know already."

The lower classes, however, are not the only people about whom she considers herself an authority. She feels equally knowledgeable about the entire social system, which she conceives as arranged according to the amount of property and wealth one possesses. "Most colored people" in her system share the bottom rank with "white-trash."

What Mrs. Turpin finally learns is that God demands a humbling of anyone who feels superior. This wisdom is given her in a vision in which she sees "a vast swinging bridge extending upward from the earth through a field of living fire." What she sees on the bridge is startling indeed: "Upon it a vast horde of souls were rumbling toward heaven. There were whole companies of white-trash, clean for the first time in their lives, and bands of black niggers in white robes, and battalions of freaks and lunatics. . . . And bringing up the end of the procession was a tribe of people . . . like herself and Claud."

This isn't to say we should see O'Connor as calling for an egalitarian society. Indeed, in this story as well as the others, she presents the whole idea of a reversal of the social order as absurd. But it is precisely the absurdity of it all that reveals what O'Connor appears to consider a basic truth: that there is no justice on earth. In fact, the whole idea of a completely altered social system seems as repugnant to O'Connor as it is to her characters.

And yet, more often than not, it is her "poor whites" who bring redemption to the others. It is they who are the bearers of "truth" about the absurdity and "rottenness of life" and the Calvinistic depravity of man. They are also sometimes given a sense of true communion with other human beings—as evidenced in "The Artificial Nigger"—that is denied the middle-class characters who face the brutality of the world completely alienated, until they are awakened by a revelation.

O'Connor's stories suggest the basic assumption that one must first experience misery to receive God's mercy. And since blacks and "poor whites" experience misery as a daily diet, they gain entrance into Paradise more readily than do their more prosperous neighbors. For this reason, it seems, O'Connor does not wish to tamper with the social system, for to create a just society would be to alter the very plan set up by the Creator.

This theme is illustrated in an early story, "The Barber," about the frustrations of a well-meaning political liberal who seeks to change the class situation for the betterment of the unfortunate. A similar character is given a more serious treatment in a later story, "The Lame Shall Enter First" about a misguided, if stereotyped reformer ironically named Sheppard, who neglects his own son while he tries to rescue a poor young ex-reformatory inmate he has witnessed eating from a trash can. He invites the boy to live in his home.

Sheppard sees the boy as deprived and in need of a chance, and masochistically accepts repeated insults and mockery, viewing these as merely "part of the boy's defensive mechanism," never flinching in his kindness until the boy finally and completely betrays his confidence through a reversion to the acts of burglary that had sent him to the reformatory in the first place.

All along, the young thief sees Sheppard as naive and accuses him of trying to play the role of Jesus Christ. He tries to be good yet "he ain't right." In the meantime, Sheppard's son, whom he has neglected, commits suicide.

Reformers, O'Connor seems to be saying, are contrary to what God wants. "I eat out of garbage cans because I like to eat out of garbage cans," the boy says, reflecting Mrs. Turpin's statement regarding "trash": "Help them you must, but help them you couldn't."

"I am very much afraid," O'Connor wrote, "that to the fiction writer the fact that we shall always have the poor with us is a source of satisfaction, for it means, essentially, that he will always find someone like himself. His concern with poverty is with a poverty fundamental to man" (qtd. in Franzen 54).

# 15

## Eudora Welty:
## The Dispossessed as Malevolent Simpleton

Welty, in *The Eye of the Story*, writes a spirited defense of her favorite author, Jane Austen. Noting that Austen's life was "unique" and her experiences "limited," Welty asks, "Will the future treat her as blindly as we have been known to treat her and take her down because she was a spinster who—having never lived anywhere outside her father's rectory and the later family homes . . . could never have got to know very much about life? Will they wish to call her a snob" (4-5)?

What follows is insightful criticism of the earlier novelist. But considering the striking parallels to Welty's own life in the facts she gives about Austen, it is hard to avoid feeling that this is as much a defense of her own work as it is of Austen's. The reason for this is that Welty has been charged with the same thing in regard to her treatment of "poor white" characters like Fay McKelva and Bonnie Dee Peacock, and she has defended herself in as spirited a fashion as she here defends Austen.

It isn't hard to imagine that Welty has been sensitive to such attacks from the very beginning, in particular Diana Trilling's early review of *Delta Wedding* that accused her of attempting to make the Fairchilds' snobbery "charming." When, some years later, Jan Norby Gretlund brought up the charge of class bias with a remark that "it has been suggested that you're 'looking down your nose'" at "poor white" characters, the usually demure Welty appears to have bristled. "That's absurd!" she replied. "I understand them very well indeed. I love them. I know just what's going on in their minds" (198).

A number of critics have agreed with Welty. Cleanth Brooks, for one, has written that "her knowledge of the way in which the southern countryman (whether sturdy yeoman or down-at-heels subsistence farmer) thinks and talks . . . bespeaks a fascination with, and a loving attention to, the rural whites of the South. She never degrades or dehumanizes them by reducing them to stereo-type." Brooks doesn't deny that such major characters as Wanda Fay, whom he calls "a shallow little vulgarian," might be seen as one-sided, but he defends Welty's portrayal as individualized and not meant to represent "poor whites" as a whole. As an example of Welty's fairness, he sights the Dalzells who are portrayed, he says, as "primitive, unlettered, and earthy in their thought and speech, but . . . not sleazily cheap" ("The Past" 578).

Another interesting defense of Welty has been done by Thomas H. Landess, who justifies her portrayals of disadvan-taged whites by making of her a regional, not a national, writer. He admits that "some of Miss Welty's most memorable characters are, in a sense, viewed down the nose of the author," but he argues that these characterizations are not "calculated to exploit the sensibilities of the culturally oppressed." Welty, he maintains, is writing from a rich and respectable tradition shared by her readers—a tradition some critics do not share and thus do not appreciate (547, 543-44).

It is just such a tradition, however, that Trilling objects to in that it creates a sense of "cultural superiority . . . which more and more comes to govern our culture—the need for satisfaction in our endemic quest for advantage, for privilege"—a need Trilling assigns not only to southerners but to all Americans. Writers like Welty, she says, form "an exclusive club" with their readers and viewers, assuring each other that they are "in" while those other people are "out" (218-19).

But what is it that is going on in the minds of "rednecks" that Welty assumes she knows? It would appear from her interviews and fiction that she believes they lack a sense of tradition that is essential to the true southerner. She told John Griffin Jones, for example, that her characters Wanda Fay McKelva and Bonnie Dee Peacock lack a memory because they don't understand their expe-rience enough to incorporate it into a memory. "If they had a memory," she said, "it would've taught them something about the present. They have nothing to draw on. They don't understand their own experience." Here, as elsewhere, Welty appears to exclude such people from being called southerners at all, when she explains: "The southerner, the Mississippian, has got a charac-ter that does stem from his sense of place and the significance of history and so on. . . . It's just a sense of continuity that has always characterized us, I think; a knowledge of family stories, that sense of generations and continuity. That gives us an identity" (28-31).

It is significant that Welty's idol Jane Austen never presumed to enter the minds of characters beneath her "station," but instead directed her satire at those either equal to or above her on the social ladder. Thus she cannot be charged with looking down her nose at the lower class. This is a crucial difference between the two writers.

Brooks is right, of course, in asserting that Welty's fiction contains sympathetic portrayals of disadvantaged whites, but these are in early stories written in the 1930s when such portraits were more prevalent in American fiction. These stories, in fact, have a Depression era feel about them that her later, more typical writing does not. It is in that later writing that she creates her devastating "poor white" characterizations.

Welty's remarks on her use of point-of-view show the actual distance between her and her lower-class subjects, a distance she felt made no difference in her ability to see inside their minds, arguing that the act of writing could erase the barrier between her experience and theirs: "I began writing from a distance, but 'Death of a Traveling Salesman' led me closer. It drew me toward what was the center of it, to a cabin back in the red clay hills— perhaps such a house as I used to see from far off on a train at night, with the firelight or lamplight showing yellow from its open doorway. In writing the story I approached and went inside" (*One Writers Beginnings* 87).

Here Welty shatters a precept of another of her favorite authors, Chekhov, who insisted that a writer never describe a place the likes of which he has not actually experienced, for otherwise he runs the risk of losing authenticity. "A lie in fiction," he wrote, "is a hundred times more boring than a lie in a conversation" (qtd. in Magershack 132).

But while Welty describes the inside of such a cabin in "Death of a Traveling Salesman," which is her first published story, she does not at this point enter the minds of the couple who inhabit the cabin, rendering all of their actions and dialogue through the perspective of the traveling salesman, whose experience would have been closer to her own. In this way she maintains an authorial distance, recording the salesman's reaction to the couple, a reaction that leads him to a frightening revelation about his own aloneness.

And yet, by venturing inside a cabin she had witnessed from a far distance, she was able to create only idealized hill folk, characterizations she might have gleaned from numerous novels popular at the time, but which do not come alive in any realistic sense. She does, nonetheless, paint a sympathetic picture of the couple as essentially contented in their natural setting. Their serenity, in fact, creates the conflict because it contrasts so sharply with the alienation of the urban-dweller Bowman.

In "A Piece of News," published a year later, Welty ventures further inside the lives of her lower-class characters. Here the outsider-protagonist is removed and we see, firsthand, the "lonesome and slow" Ruby Fisher, a "poor white" who, unlike the later Fay McKelva, has a sense of her own past and a highly developed imagination that allows her to create a scene in her mind of her husband killing her and "standing over her, as he once looked, with his wild black hair hanging to his shoulders." She also imagines him looking down at her corpse at the funeral and weeping "with some repentance" (*Collected Stories* 12, 14-15). As the story ends, Ruby and her husband demonstrate a capacity to come to realizations about themselves and their lives that Welty later pointedly denies Fay McKelva.

"The Whistle," written during the same period, is also a sympathetic treatment of a rural "poor white" couple whose "lives were filled with tiredness" because of "poverty that had bound them like a disaster" (58). Their conflict is with the natural elements in their desperate attempt to stay warm but it is also with the man who owns the land—land that they themselves had owned at one time.

The climax reminds one of tragically ironic stories by Caldwell and others of the 1930s as the freezing couple remove their own garments to cover the boss's tomato plants, then burn their own furniture in a futile attempt to stay alive. Welty's attitude parallels Caldwell's here in seeing them as victims of the sharecropping system. W.U. McDonald, Jr., has, through a textual analysis of Welty's revisions of the story, shown that an earlier version published in *Prairie Schooner* "contains a number of circumstantial details about the operation of the sharecropper system," details she deleted from the story as it appears in *A Curtain of Green* so that she could further develop the whistle "as a symbol of the system and its consequences for human beings" (193).

The significant thing is that in this early story, Welty gives her "poor white" protagonist a sense of the past as well as a vivid imagination and sensibility that allows her to notice "the colors of the green and red, the smell of the sun on the ground, the touch of leaves and of warm ripening tomatoes" (*Collected Stories* 58). It is difficult indeed to imagine Fay McKelva noticing such things in the first place, let alone savoring their image.

This story seems quaintly tied to its time, however, the reason probably that, as Louise Westling has noted, Welty's "experience of traveling through the eighty-two counties of Mississippi [as a WPA publicity agent] taught her how protected her life had been." But she separates Welty from other, more socially committed writers of the day in that, rather than seeing the poor "as sociological data or political victims, she approached them with a sense of kinship and admiration for the spirit with which they lived their difficult lives" (63).

However true this may be of these early stories, it is not true of Welty's later fiction. "The Hitch-Hikers," for example, prepares us for more typical portraits: here we have stereotypical country bumpkins, one of whom describes his home in the hills where "we had us owls for chickens and fox for yard dogs but we sung true," and another who hits his guitar-playing partner over the head with a beer bottle because "I was just tired of him always uppin' an' makin' a noise about everything" (71).

Welty's movement from sympathy for such characters in her earlier stories to revulsion in the later fiction is actually predicted in another story from her first collection called "A Memory." The story is told in the first person from the point-of-view of a young girl who has a burning need to "watch everything" that happens around her. She is a budding artist who has developed the habit of viewing people she encounters as subjects for her art, actually framing them with her hands in the way of a painter. She is also prone to pass "judgment upon every person and every event." In addition, she has the artist's tendency to idealize life: "When a person, or a happening, seemed to me not in keeping with my opinion, or even my hope or expectation, I was terrified by a vision of abandonment and wildness which tore my heart with a kind of sorrow" (75).

As a budding writer, she also views people and happenings as stories. She remembers, for instance, a boy she has never talked to but who, in a brief encounter on the school stairs, accidentally brushed her wrist. The incident has probably been forgotten by the boy, but the girl dramatizes it in her mind until it emerges as a "very long story" that she recaptures in her mind again and again (77).

Reality intrudes when she observes a group of "squirming ill-sorted people" on the beach whose "old and faded bathing suits" reveal thick, misshapen bodies. They are, in her eyes, "common" and "not at all the sort of bathers she would have liked to have around her," and they force her to realize the existence of a world outside of her imagination, a world where ugliness exists. Her dilemma is compounded by the fact that the bathers seem to be "resigned to each other's daring and ugliness." And when one of them, a young man, turns to look at her, she is "stunned," feeling that he has, with his look and smile, effectively included her in their world. At this point she wishes "they were all dead." She immediately closes her eyes to blot them out (77-78).

Yet the vivid imagery of their "ugly bodies" cavorting in the sand stays with her, obliterating the romantic image of the boy at school. And although she tries again and again to revive it, "the memory itself did not come to me." Instead there is an altered, more realistic image of a "medium-sized boy with blond hair, his unconscious eyes looking beyond me and out the window, solitary and unprotected" (79-80).

This story not only beautifully illustrates an adolescent awakening from innocence but convincingly depicts an artist's attempt to reconcile ugliness with a previously conceived idealized vision of life. The story also illustrates a transition in Welty's fiction from a romanticized view of lower-class characters to what she seems to feel is a more realistic one. It conveys, as well, the dilemma of a protected child whose experience has included neither economic deprivation nor any real contact with people outside of her own class.

One might project from this that when such a person grows up and writes fiction, she is apt to see such people sympathetically only from a distance, as from the window of a train. When she moves "inside" such people, without having shared their experiences of poverty, she is apt to concentrate on their ugliness and to rely on long-established stereotypes to explain their behavior.

Welty's remarks in the essay on Jane Austen come into focus at this point. The writer, she tells us, needs an audience that shares her vision and her values. And when one reads Katherine Anne Porter's description of "A Petrified Man" as offering "a fine clinical study" of "individuals exactly and clearly presented" (xxi), Ruth M. Vande Kieft's characterization of the same story as a faithful rendering of "attitudes, modes of behavior and speech of one level of modern American society" (65), and Landess's remark that "Miss Welty, in several of her most successful works, has focused on characters whose tackiness can only be described as ingenious" (554), one can see that Welty has indeed received the audience she desired.

Sympathetic critics have also charged Welty's detractors with not being able to face the truth about lower-class people. Such a charge is implicit in J.A. Bryant's comment that if some characters in Welty are "unsavory, they are nevertheless real; and like other forms of truth, they properly evoke a mixed response" (7). Welty herself has asserted that the true novelist seeks only "to show, to disclose" and that "his persuasions are all toward allowing his reader to see and hear something for himself" (*The Eye of the Story* 149).

But writers, no matter how objective, do not simply record life, for the details they choose to include, as well as the details they choose not to include, present to the reader a selected perspective on life, determined by the predisposition of the writer. Welty, in fact, says as much in another passage from the same volume that seems to contradict the statement above: "It is through the shaping of the work in the hands of the artist that you most nearly come to know what can be known, on the page, of his mind and heart, and his as apart from the others. No other saw life in an ordering exactly like him. So shape begins and ends subjectively" (144).

Robbie, the runaway wife in *Delta Wedding* (1945) is a case in point. An early prototype of the Fay McKelva character in *The Optimist's Daughter*, she misses being a stereotype as Welty gives her ample motivation for her actions, which includes a justifiable resentment of the Fairchilds, as well as shame at having to accept their paternalistic charity in the form of hand-me-down clothes and payment for her high school education. Additional motivation comes from her understandable reluctance to be pulled into this close-knit family, especially since they are either laughing at her "in the presence of comparative strangers" or accusing her of marrying for money. "We are an unfair people," Shelley Fairchild confides in her diary. "We are all such sweet people to be so spoiled" (161, 85).

This sentiment is seemingly shared by Welty since the family undergoes no change in this respect throughout the novel. The only change seems to be their final acceptance of the protagonist, Laura, as a member of the family, but this only after she has undergone a long initiation into their "tricks" and exclusionary tactics (74).

The family's exclusiveness, moreover, seems to shut out everyone who has not been born into it. For example, Ellen, the mother who has given birth to all the Fairchild children, still feels locked out of the inner circle. She even suspects that Uncle George, who is now the chief male figure in the family and thus the focus of this paternalistically organized family's attention, is "in reality, not intimate with this household at all, and they did not know it" (81).

Even the practice of "marrying down" engaged in by Uncle George, Uncle Pinck, and Dabney, seems more than anything an attempt to break the exclusiveness, although, as Landess says, the only thing that seems to come from the inclusion of their lower-class spouses into the family is "a certain loss of social grace" (554).

John Edward Hardy correctly sees George's wife Robbie's "peasant cruelty [as] undeniable," but points out "the callousness of the whole Fairchild family" toward her. "The total portrait," he writes, "is one of a woman who is at least the equal of any of the Fairchild women in moral character and very possibly their superior in emotional integrity and stamina" (96).

But what are we to make of the "radiant" ending when Laura gleefully embraces these "unfair" people, becoming in George's words, "a real little Fairchild," especially since this seems to come about solely because at long last they agree to let her into their exclusive circle? Are we to see this only as the sincere and understandable desire of an orphan to be accepted by a family? Or are we to rejoice with Laura in her acceptance into this particular family and to find them admirable?

It is Welty's seeming approval of the Fairchilds and her desire that we find them acceptable that has brought the charge of snobbery against her in this novel. On the other hand, it seems to be the reluctance of some critics to believe that Welty actually wants us to like this family that has brought the charge that the novel is opaque.

But given the final paragraph of the novel, it would seem that we are indeed to approve of the family and to rejoice in Laura's acceptance into it. Hardy, who assumes that the Fairchilds have "class superiority," reasons that they can get away with bad behavior toward others because they are "rich . . . in the life of the mind and sensibilities" and thus have "grace" and "style beyond manners" (94). But, as Jane Austen might say, manners are the determining factor in judging behavior and manners are what the Fairchilds most lack.

The theme of the novel therefore seems not opaque at all. For if we are to accept Welty's statement, cited earlier, that a true southern family's sensibility entails a "sense of place . . . generations . . . [and] continuity," and if we add to this the family's right to exclude, even be abusive toward, outsiders they believe do not possess those qualities, then we must agree that the Fairchilds are a family any true southerner would be happy to join. My guess is that most southerners would not, that they would instead deem Jane Austen's notion of "polite performance" more important than exclusivity.

In *The Ponder Heart* (1953), we again see Welty's theme of lower-class females marrying into families "above" their social station, but here Welty's judgment of such intruders is harsher than it had been in *Delta Wedding*. Her portrait of Bonnie Dee Peacock is more scathing and more stereotypical than that of Robbie Fairchild, for in *Ponder Heart*, motivation for "trashy" behavior has essentially disappeared. Bonnie Dee is "trashy" solely because of "her origins" (49). Thus the comic descriptions of her mother as "big and fat as a row of pigs" and her father as having "a face as red as a Tom Turkey and not a tooth to his name." Welty even borrows from the comedian Minnie Pearl to give the mother a new pair of pants with "the tag still poking out the seam" (87). Moreover, this family, in stereotypical "hillbilly" fashion, does not mind "hearing how lazy they were" (96).

One aspect of the narrator Edna Earle's humor that is particularly disturbing is her making fun of things that disadvantaged rural people do out of necessity, such as keeping worn-out appliances on their premises. Rural residents have not received many of the services city-dwellers take for granted, such as the hauling off of trash. In the country, disposing of worn-out appliances is an expensive operation and one subsistence farmers can ill afford. There is also a real need to keep the old appliance around for parts to keep its secondhand replacement in operation. This, of course, ties into J. Wayne Flynt's point, made earlier, that subsistence farmers have long lived by "an ethic of repair or mend." Insult is added to injury, however, when Welty has Bonnie Dee haul her *working* washing machine to the porch of the Ponder mansion.

Another activity of the Peacock family that Edna Earle finds amusing is their waving at passing trains every chance they get. This is actually a charming practice, as is the tradition in rural areas of waving at passing motorists, whether one knows them or not. Both activities indicate a sense of community that Welty goes out of her way to praise in "better" southern families but which she claims is missing in families such as the Peacocks.

Yet another practice that Edna Earle finds amusing is Mrs. Peacock's constant wearing of bedroom slippers. She seems unaware that many poor women have had to wear cheap, ill-fitting shoes for so many years that they have ruined their feet and can find nothing but bedroom slippers bearable.

Cleanth Brooks has called *Losing Battles* (1970) Welty's "most profound and most powerfully moving account of the folk society" ("Eudora Welty" 102), and it is obvious that Welty considers the Renfros closer to the "yeoman" category than to "poor white trash"—although why the rest of the family simply gives up and lets the farm go to ruin when young Jack goes off to jail is not explained. It is also obvious, however, that in this novel, each character, whether high or low on the social scale, is treated equally. The Renfros, the Judge, and Mrs. Moody are all made to appear ridiculous.

There are several instances in the novel, however, which can be seen as lapses of taste on the part of the narrator—for example, the prolonged episode wherein Jack and Gloria, as they ramble down a hill, toss their eighteen-month-old baby back and forth through the air, catching it "like a basketball," which would break any baby's neck. Also objectionable are Welty's descriptions of the same baby as having legs "like a frog" and "bellowing" (120, 185, 119).

But it is in *The Optimist's Daughter* (1972) that Welty gives perhaps her most devastating portrait of a lower-class character in Wanda Fay McKelva who is simply mean, selfish, and cruel, without motivation except for her "poor white trash" background. She has absolutely no redeeming qualities. She even spits at Laurel when Laurel tells her that her husband, who is also Laurel's father, has died. And when she sits at the gravesite, instead of mourning, she busily pats her hair into place (35, 92).

In the climax of the novel—the fight over the breadboard—Welty gives us the theme summed up by Laurel in her realization that she is, in fact, morally superior to Fay because she has "powers of passion and imagination" that Fay does not have. She also has the ability, absent in Fay, to wed her experience of the past with that of the present to assure the continuity so necessary to the southerner. "The past isn't a thing to me," Fay screams at Laurel in Snopes fashion. "I belong to the future, didn't you know that" (179).

Fay's family, one of whom is stereotypically named Bubba, receive equally condescending treatment. The Dalzells fare no better. A female of that family wears bedroom slippers all the way from Texas to New Orleans, in the manner of Mrs. Peacock, and then proceeds to sit in the hospital waiting room holding a "half-eaten banana," monkey-fashion, while the relative she has come to see dies in another room. At the same time, the dying man's son stretches out on a sofa, drinks himself into a stupor, and snores loudly.

No doubt we are meant to see both, as we are meant to see the Snopes clan, as a species of human beings near the bottom of the evolutionary scale. When we couple this with Fay's statement that she belongs to the future, we can see a further parallel to Faulkner—as well as to William Gilmore Simms and the Southwest humorists—and that is Welty's apparent fear that these people constitute a definite threat to the established order and to values she holds most dear. This might go a long toward explaining Welty's often condescending portrayals of her lower-class characters.

# 16

## Cormac McCarthy:
## The Dispossessed as Naked Ape

Critics, with few exceptions, have granted Cormac McCarthy a prominent, if not exalted place in American letters. Deemed "brilliant" (Arnold and Luce 4) and "extraordinarily gifted" (Sullivan 661), he has received praise equal to, if not exceeding that given Faulkner. One reviewer, for example, has rendered McCarthy's *Child of God* a reading experience "so intense, so . . . religious, as to elude description" (Grumback). Another has given McCarthy credit for a "wise" and "compassionate" understanding of human nature (Davenport).[1]

Many of these panegyrics seem to have been written in the heat of the moment, and perhaps their authors have since had second thoughts. Nonetheless, such praise in influential periodicals has served to establish McCarthy's current reputation among scholars and general readers as one of our foremost American writers.

A careful reevaluation of his southern fiction will, however, show that his tooth-and-claw world vision is neither compassionate nor wise, but rather warmed-over nineteenth-century Social Darwinism. It will further show that many of his characterizations are neither sympathetic nor dispassionate, as has been claimed, but rather some of the most blatant stereotypes of southern "rednecks" in contemporary American fiction.

McCarthy differs from most writers in that he does not seem interested in his characters' actions within society, but rather outside of it, his attempt apparently being to show them as allegorical humanity, inhabiting a Hobbesian world of collision and conflict, a world where survival does not depend on thought processes but rather on the instinctual drive to overpower one's fellow creatures. This may be why McCarthy has garnered such an avid following, for he very pointedly projects an image of people as extremely isolated, alienated, violent, and amoral—an image present-day readers might understandably accept as true.

A basic problem, however, is that the tooth-and-claw view of nature McCarthy depicts has been discarded by scientists for most of this century. One might wonder where he acquired it. A possible answer might be found in a group of widely circulated "scientific" studies published during the time he was getting his start as a writer, the 1960s. These bestsellers—Konrad Lorenz's *On Aggression*, Robert Ardrey's *The Territorial Imperative*, Anthony Storr's *Human Aggression*, and Desmond Morris's *The Naked Ape*—were widely read during the period, serving to briefly revive the nineteenth-century theory, at least among nonscientists.

In fact, McCarthy's protagonist Lester Ballard's intuitive sense in *Child of God* (1973) that "all things" fight (169) can easily be seen as anticipated by Lorenz's phenomenally popular *On Aggression*, whose subject, according to the author, was "the fighting instinct in beast and man" (ix). Moreover, McCarthy's Neanderthal-like cannibals in *Outer Dark* (1968) who roam the woods searching for victims, slaughtering and eating a human baby, appear to be fictional manifestations of Lorenz's since-discredited prototype of ancient humanity "who learned to preserve fire [and] used it to roast his brothers," engaging in "the occasional taking of the heads of women and children encountered in the woods" (231, 242).[2]

This is not the only instance of erroneous reporting of scientific findings by Lorenz and the others, as scientists of the day tried to alert the public. Critics of Ardrey's *The Territorial Imperative*, for example, noted at the time that the author was not a scientist but a playwright, and Lorenz's fellow ethologist, J.P. Scott, wrote that Lorenz had not taken into account "most of the scientific discoveries of the past 50 years" (137). But these pronouncements went unheard by the vast reading public.

Psychologist Leonard Berkowitz accounted for this phenomenon in his 1969 article, "Simple Views of Aggression." The reason the books were so popular in the 1960s was, he said, that they offered "easy formulas" to what the public perceived as the overriding human dilemma of the time—humanity's apparently aggressive nature. The explanations offered by these books helped to "relieve the anxiety born of the public's concern with war, social unrest, race riots and student protest" (39).

Apparently in response to this anxiety, McCarthy set out to illustrate the thesis developed by Lorenz and the others by creating characters like the mass-murderer Lester Ballard in *Child of God* who represents not merely a dispossessed farmer, but, in reference to the title of that novel, all humankind. Moreover, McCarthy seems to feel that such a character need not be motivated in the usual sense, for if aggregate humanity can be explained in Lorenzian terms, what need is there for purely individual motivation?

There are many readers, of course, who believe in the existence of unadulterated evil in human nature, which in turn leads to a belief in the need for humanity to either submit to some form of absolutist government—such as the secular monarchy of Hobbes—or to find redemption in a force outside of nature, such as a supreme being. Such readers do not always demand psychological motivation beyond humanity's basically corrupt nature; in fact, the insertion of individualized motivation often disrupts what they feel should be the central theme of literature, that is, humanity's need for subjugation to either an earthly or a supernatural power, or both.

But McCarthy doesn't seem to offer a political or religious option, or if he does, it is well concealed. His fiction, however, seems to operate on the level of allegory; but without the ultimate appeal to secular or religious authority, one wonders what McCarthy's allegory alludes to, if anything.

Further, the question remains as to whether McCarthy has effectively bridged the gap between realism and allegory. For those very qualities that are assets to his fiction—his ear for speech and mannerisms, his capacity for rendering vivid realistic detail—tend to pull his characters out of allegory, where they might be safely seen as archetypes, to the realm of realistic fiction, where they become stereotypes.

In *The Orchard Keeper* (1965), McCarthy hints at the type of figure that will dominate his future fiction, even anticipating the title of his next novel in his characterization of Kenneth Rattner, a man so alienated from society, he is constantly "seeking . . . that being in the outer dark with whom only he held communion, smiling a little to himself, the onlooker, the stranger" (24).

We see McCarthy's Lorenzian theme developed to a fuller extent in *Outer Dark*, especially in the passages where three mysterious killers roam the countryside. The black-haired leader, attired ominously in a black suit, slits a baby's throat and belly and gives it to his companion to eat, for no other reason, it seems, than that he is completely depraved. And, as if to add cruelty of authorial attitude to cruelty of character, the omniscient narrator describes the baby just prior to its being slaughtered as "dangling . . . like a dressed rabbit . . . one eye opening and closing softly like a naked owl's" (235-36).

In his next novel, *Child of God* (1973), McCarthy creates the ultimate outsider in the necrophiliac mass murderer Lester Ballard. He does, however, establish a partial motive for Ballard's revenge on humanity in that he is evicted from his farm; his motivation is further explained by a neighbor who tells us that "he never was right after his daddy killed hisself." Moreover, his terrible loneliness and alienation from normal human existence is established when he first rapes a female corpse and "pours into that waxen ear everything he'd ever thought of saying to a woman" (21, 88).

But these hardly account for his becoming a mass murderer who carries his victims into caves where he stores their bodies, pausing now and then to copulate with the females. Nor does McCarthy mean for us to take these as sufficient motivation, for he goes out of his way to portray Ballard as an archetypal scapegoat "sustained by his fellow men. . . . a race that gives suck to the maimed and the crazed, that wants this wrong blood in its history and will have it" (4, 156). The insertion of this thesis suggests the Social Darwinist contention that the physically and mentally maimed should not be sustained by either public or private charity but should instead be allowed to die off as a part of a natural evolutionary process.

Ballard's extreme alienation from society forces him further into the world of nature where he enters a valley and watches "the diminutive progress of all things" which appear to him so "lovely" that he lets "his head drop between his knees and he begins to cry" (127). That this natural world he feels so close to is one of eternal violence and conflict is evident when he watches hounds chase a boar and overtake him, at which time the boar turns on them, disemboweling one. McCarthy clearly does not wish his reader to be repulsed by this image, but rather to see the beauty of nature "tooth and claw": "He watched this ballet tilt and swirl and churn mud up through the snow and watched the lovely blood welter there in its holograph of battle, spray burst from a ruptured lung, the dark heart's blood" (69).

McCarthy also sees his protagonist as having reverted to his anthropoidal background, as he sits in his cave, "gibbering a sound not quite crying that echoes from the walls of the grotto like the mutterings of a band of sympathetic apes" (159).

What provides a great deal of the unevenness in these two novels is not only McCarthy's wavering from allegory to realism but his dipping into comic stereotypes of disadvantaged and dispossessed white southerners as well. This is evident in his first novel, *The Orchard Keeper*, which only hints at the Lorenzian theme he develops later, but nonetheless contains extremely broad stereotypes, such as this description of a group of families as

gaunt hollow-eyed and darkskinned people . . . who reproduced with such frightening prolificness that their entire lives appeared devoted to the production of the ragged line of scions which shoeless and tattered sat for hours on the porch edges, themselves not unlike the victims of some terrible disaster and stared out across the blighted land with expressions of neither hope nor wonder nor despair. (12)

If the thematic and stylistic Faulkner influences here are too readily apparent, the source of some of his humor seems to spring from the comic strip "Snuffy Smith," especially the episode in which liquor-guzzling hillfolk sit stupidly in the Green Fly Inn, which is "built on a scaffolding of poles over a sheer drop" and whose "one corner was nailed to a pine tree that rose towering out of the hollow." On windy nights, these dim-witted mountaineers "trod floors that waltzed drunkenly beneath them, surged and buckled with huge groans. At times the whole building would careen madly to one side as though headlong into collapse," at which point the drinkers would pause briefly, then return to their talk and liquor. At one crucial point the porch actually falls into the gap, carrying with it a group of the drinkers, after which, "torn" and "unclothed," they crawl out of the precipice, reenter the inn, and immediately fall upon each other, "murderously" fighting into the night (12-13, 25).

McCarthy is also fond of Faulkner's practice of rendering rural whites in animal imagery, comparing, for example, a group of farm boys to "curious birds," another to cows, and Rattner's wife to a toad (16, 18, 61). He further describes a principal character, Marion Sylder, as "courting with ribald humor the country slatterns that hung on the city's perimeter," experimenting with one of them by wetting his finger to "cut a white streak on the grime" of her neck. He also assumes, like Caldwell, that young "poor white" females love to copulate with any man who comes along. Sylder and his friend June, for example, stop along the road and proceed to "screw" two passing girls—one in an empty church and one in an outhouse (29, 21).

McCarthy does, however, create characters in this novel that are, to various degrees, sympathetic. One such character is the boy John Wesley Rattner, the son of a degenerate tenant farmer who, in Sartie Snopes fashion, breaks away from his family's influence at the end of the novel. He is given various episodes that demonstrate a sensitivity that separates him from his father. One is his finding a young rabbit in a well and attempting to keep it alive by tossing down lettuce leaves until at last the rabbit dies. Another is his encountering a wounded sparrow hawk on the road and unsuccessfully attempting to nurse it back to life (63-64, 77). He is also not stereotyped as lazy, as we see in this passage: "He cut wood, went out early to the rising stacks of new pine kindling. . . . He worked hard at it." Some heroic stature is even added when he rescues Sylder from a car wreck (72, 112).

Unfortunately, John Wesley's characterization becomes completely sentimentalized when, in the final episode, he visits his mother's grave site, touches the gravestone, and realizes he owes allegiance to an old man who has been kind to him, rather than to his despicable father.

The old man to whom he owes allegiance is Arthur Ormsby, another sentimental character whose actions and thought are frequently cliché-ridden. He is, in fact, a "hillbilly" Thoreau, with a touch of Yeats thrown in, who shuns humanity to sit on his porch with one foot tapping out "the tune of some old ballad" while he studies "the movements of stars," an old hound dog by his side (20): "If I was a younger man, he told himself, I would move to them mountains. I would find me a clearwater branch and build me a log house with a fireplace. And my bees would make black mountain honey. And I wouldn't care for no man. Then I wouldn't be unneighborly neither, he added" (55).

A touch of what appears at first to be sensitivity is revealed when, as a teenager, he and some neighbor boys pass a house and see, through the window, a woman undressing for bed. When the others go back "for a second look," he does not and they laugh at him. The old man, however, remembers this episode "with dim regret," possibly feeling now that he has missed out on an aspect of life that would have been nice to experience, but it is not apparent otherwise that he ever needs or desires a woman (89).

His involvement with John Wesley comes about through his insistence on maintaining his isolation. For when he comes upon the dead body of the boy's father, he proceeds to cover it up and then to shield it for the next seven years, presumably to keep others away from his property. He also proves to be the perfect host when John Wesley comes to his cabin to visit, which accounts for the boy's allegiance.

In *Outer Dark*, McCarthy creates not only a Faulknerian wilderness landscape, but two characters who are reminiscent of Lena Grove and Byron Bunch, albeit stripped of the latter couple's humorous aspects and capacity for even elementary thought. McCarthy's characters never rise above such primitive observations as "I'd admire to have me a drink of that there fresh spring water" and "I bet I ain't eat two pones of lightbread in my life" (28, 60). The fact that they are brother and sister introduces the much overworked theme of incest into an already totally bleak picture of humanity.

As the novel opens, the sister is giving birth to a baby in an isolated cabin where she and her brother have taken up temporary quarters. When the baby arrives, the brother takes it out and buries it in a shallow grave, although it is still alive. It is found by a passing tinker who pokes "a finger at it as one might a tomato or melon," then carries it down the road to a woman who agrees to care for it (20-22).

The further Faulknerian traveling-down-the-road theme is introduced when the brother, Culla Holme, leaves the cabin looking for work and the sister, Rinthey, waking up alone and not knowing where her brother has gone, takes off down the road "a-huntin' that tinker," asking from house to house and store to store, telling the people that the tinker has stolen "somethin' belonged to me" (54, 60). The brother spends the bulk of the novel, in turn, looking for his sister.

Faulkner's penchant for rendering the Snopes clan in animal imagery is once more indulged by McCarthy in his descriptions of these disadvantaged whites. Holme's "eyeballs," for example, tilt "like a toad's," and a boy's mouth snaps "open like a turtle's." As if to compound the imagery, one old woman is described as various animals at once, peering "sideways at the others like a cowled mandrill" who "lost her beak" when "a stovepipe . . . fell and sliced her off slick as . . . a frog's belly." Another character, reminiscent of Ike Snopes, is described as having a sexual preference for "she-hogs." Yet another emerges from a "slattern shack," appearing as a "hooded anthropoid" with "an aged face and . . . hair all hung in clots like a sheep's scut" (175, 69, 216, 109).

The references to anthropoids and mandrills, of course, place the characters at an early stage on the evolutionary scale and help to establish them as near-representations of prehumans, a theme carried even further in the description of an itinerant family that "could have been stone figures quarried from the architecture of an older time" (77).

Moreover, throughout this novel, dispossessed rural whites are, for the most part, presented in the most stereotypical forms possible—for example, "the toothless old woman who bent near-sightedly into her plate with smacking gums, a sparse tuft of long white chin hairs wagging and drifting above the food," or the boy who stands with "his hands deep in the rear pockets of his trousers, scraping his feet on the ground like a man who has stepped in manure." The latter description once more recalls Faulkner (60, 63). There is also a good bit of stereotyping in *Child of God*, principally in the "dumpkeeper" and the nine daughters he has "spawned," who appear to have emerged from *God's Little Acre* only to be tainted by further grotesqueness. "Gangling progeny with black hair hanging from their armpits," they sit "idle and wide-eyed day after day in chairs and crates about the little yard" blinking "their sluggard lids," pursued by "lanky country boys with long cocks and big feet." McCarthy adds:

They moved like cats and like cats in heat attracted surrounding swains to their midden until the old man used to go out at night and fire a shotgun at random just to clear the air. . . . They were coming and going all hours in all manner of degenerate cars, a dissolute carousel of rotting sedans and *niggerized* convertibles [italics mine]. (26-27)

The latter reference is especially offensive, coming as it does from the omniscient narrator, who rivals this racism with cruelty when he elsewhere calls an "idiot-child" a "drooling cretin" (116).

In *Suttree* (1979), McCarthy creates another dispossessed figure in Gene Harrogate, who moves from his rural home to the heart of the city and, unlike his rural counterparts in the earlier novels, engages in illegal activities without doing any real harm to other people.

Actually this character is co-protagonist, sharing that role with Cornelius Suttree, a middle-class, college-educated man who comes into contact with Harrogate when he flees from his marriage and his status-conscious father to take up residence in a houseboat on the river, renouncing his middle-class ancestry and associating exclusively with the truly dispossessed, the homeless and the destitute. The two are placed in juxtaposition so that we are made to see what McCarthy perceives to be Suttree's ever-present angst and Harrogate's equally persistent ease with his destitute condition—the former illustrating an educated person's existential condition, the latter demonstrating the innocent naivete and contentment of a simple country boy.

The two meet when Suttree is arrested for drunkenness and is thrown in jail and Harrogate, an eighteen-year-old fresh from the country, appears in Suttree's cell "crouched above his bed like a wizened bird," staring at Suttree with "witless equanimity" (54). The animal imagery is further extended to include Harrogate as a "skinned spidermonkey," "country mouse," and "city rat" (58, 92, 211). Arrested for copulating with a watermelon, and thus dubbed "the moonlight melonmaster," he sustains "incipient good will" throughout the novel (48, 42).

Unfortunately, he also takes on attributes of comic characters in numerous country-music shows, in particular when he emerges wearing a shirt "fashioned from an enormous pair of striped drawers, his neck stuck through the ripped seam of a crotch, his arms hanging from the capacious legholes like sticks." He is also the proud wearer of a pair of shoes four or five inches too long, proclaiming happily, "I cain't stand a tight shoe" (115).

His glee is sustained even though he takes up residence beneath a viaduct, noting the dust, rubble, and trash all around him, "slapping his thigh" and exclaiming, "Hot damn . . . I'll have her fixed up slick next time you see it" (118). And sure enough, he drags in some crates, old bricks, and a mattress, then catches pigeons for food, inviting Suttree for a meal. As they sit, hearing the "sewage gurgling and shuttling along through the pipes hung from the bridge's underbelly overhead," he cries out, "Slick, ain't it?" And to the African-American whose pig he has stolen, he says, "I like it down here, don't you? I mean you're close to town and all. And they don't bother ye" (137, 141). When asked if he'd like to work out the cost of the hog, he replies, "Work. It's how most folks get their livin'. Them that ain't prowlin' other folks' hogpens" (142).

Lewis Simpson gives perhaps the best justification for McCarthy's fiction in that the "dark narcissism" of characters such as Lester Ballard illustrates "a democratic solitude of the self" which, liberated "at all cost" from the community, represents a dead end. "The ultimate expense of this liberation," Simpson writes, "is not only the imprisonment of self in self but the closure of history in the self ("Southern Fiction" 189-90).

This is certainly an important theme. The pity is that it is illustrated with stereotyped characters, whether grotesque killers or comic hillbillies, and situations which make it less than convincing. How much more powerful the statement would be had it emerged through believable situations and characters.

# 17

# Harry Crews:
# The Dispossessed as Poor White Trash

Harry Crews has closer ties to disadvantaged whites than do most authors, although his repeated claim that "I was a share-cropper's son" (*Blood and Grits* 146) suggests more perhaps than is actually true. For his father, an adventurous young man, had sharecropped briefly so that he could save money to buy a piece of land and settle a black family on it, paying them wages—all of which occurred by the time Crews was twenty-one months old. At that point the father died (*A Childhood* 148-50).

This is not to say that Crews does not feel the anger and frus-tration of the "redneck"—his origins are rural and southern, and often not that far removed from abject poverty, especially when his mother was working at a cigar factory and the family was forced to accept food and clothing from charitable agencies (132-33).

But Crews himself has felt compelled to modify his own myth, at one point correcting an interviewer who innocently stated that Crews would, as a child, "eat dirt to get the minerals you needed." Crews' response: "We didn't have to eat dirt, but we did. That's not too unusual for kids to do" (Walsh 97).

All of this is important because claims have been made for Crews's expertise in writing about "poor whites." Frank W. Shel-ton, for example, has said that "Crews, to my knowledge, is absolutely unique among southern writers in that he writes about life from the perspective of the poor white. He writes from *within the class*, not observing it from without, the traditional perspective of white southern writers" (47-50). And William M. Moss cites Crews's fusing with the protagonist Joe Lon Mackey in *A Feast of Snakes* (1976) as an example of this lower-class affinity (44-45).

But, in truth, there is much in Joe Lon that is not lower-class at all. He dates the most popular cheerleader at the high school, a thing few "poor white" students would dream of doing, and his father owns a store, which places him in the hierarchy of the small town in which he lives. He elects, in fact, to stay at home and run his father's store while the cheerleader goes off to the state university—adopting one option and rejecting another, both of which have been unavailable to the poor. Moreover, he spends most of his time drinking with a lawyer from the city, who has neither the inclination or desire to pal around with sharecroppers or other "trash."

Joe Lon's problems, in fact, do not stem from a poverty background, or from lost opportunity, but rather from a deep sexual frustration and a desire to commit violence against women, all women. "You git Mama and Beeder," he tells his father, "and I'll git Elf and the babies and you and me'll git'm all in a room in the big house and we'll just beat the shit out of them. Beat 'em I said goddamit. Slap'm. Bust their faces." Their only crime: they are women. The narrator elaborates:

He did not know what love was. . . . But he knew he carried it around with him, a scabrous spot of rot, for which there was no cure. Rage would not cure it. Indulgency made it worse, inflamed it, made it grow like a cancer. The world had seemed a good and livable place. But love, love seemed to mess up everything. (118)

The one time Crews treats truly poor characters, he out-Caldwells Caldwell in characterizations more in keeping with television sitcoms of the 1960s than serious fiction. I'm speaking of those pages in *The Gospel Singer* (1968) where the protagonist visits his parents, sharecroppers who have moved off the land into a mansion paid for with the protagonist's earnings as a gospel singer. The family, in keeping with the image presented in *Beverly Hillbillies*, don't know how to behave in a real house, letting pigs track through, giving the carpet "the rancid smell of hog manure" to which the inhabitants are completely oblivious. In addition, they use chamber pots even though bathrooms are right down the hall and, echoing Dude's behavior in *Tobacco Road*, proceed to ruin the new truck their son has given them by putting water in the crankcase and oil in the radiator, after which they abandon it by leaving it in the front yard which is "choked in weeds" (62, 69-70, 61).

To top it all, they journey to Atlanta to take Gerd, "a tall, bloodless boy with chalky skin and hair the color of milk," to a doctor in order to treat his scabrous skin in much the same way Jeeter Lester takes Elly Mae to Augusta to get her harelip repaired. And like Jeeter, who forgets his mission once he's in the city, the family wander around the city, unable to find a doctor, and finally go to the movies. Gerd doesn't mind a bit. In fact, we are told, he "wouldn't have it no other way after he started goin crazy and seen that Doris Day and that Rock Hudson" (68).

Longstreet, Hooper, Harris, Caldwell, Welty, and McCarthy also created condescending portraits of dispossessed and disadvantaged whites. But Harry Crews, unlike these writers, has long sought to identify with a "redneck" heritage, having experienced the alienating effects of condescension and caricature from the middle- and upper-class segments of society. His devastating portraits of "poor whites" seem, in this respect, to be not so much condescension as self-loathing.

# Part Four:

# Overcoming the Stereotype

# 18

# The Beginnings of Something Positive

There appears to be an emerging sense in the various disciplines of social science and the humanities that dispossessed southern whites have not been treated fairly by scholars and researchers, that they have long been negatively stereotyped and viewed with a definite bias. Anthropologists and sociologists have, of late, sought to correct this image, but historical and literary scholarship has not kept pace.

But this is changing. For one thing, literary critics and historians are less apt now than formerly to have an elitist background or outlook. Secondly, thinking in the South as a whole has undergone a radical change, a process that amounts to a democratization of a once rigidly stratified society. This development is illustrated by J. Bill Berry in his essay titled "Class Southerner":

My parents were well educated and had done their best to teach me manners. But neither their backgrounds nor their values were aristocratic. Gentility was for them a code of conduct, not a pedigree. Their manners did not stem from their sense of station or depend on their perceptions of the station of others. Rather, they flowed from a democratic faith that everyone was entitled to courtesy and respect. Further, everyone was "as good as everyone else." (185)

This democratic spirit, seemingly the result of education coupled with understanding and a capacity for tolerance, has been fostered in the population as a whole through the movement of many dispossessed and disadvantaged whites into mainstream society. Once this happens to any group, it is seen in a more favorable light. This point is made by historian I.A. Newby, who in the mid-1980s called for more research into this much-maligned group:

Sea changes in the historical treatment of a social group occur in conjunction with basic improvements in the status of the group itself. The abatement of popular prejudice serves, as it were, to legitimize the group and, in the process, facilitate a new and more sympathetic look at its history. Signs of improving treatment of poor whites are numerous, in and out of historical scholarship, but the process itself is far from complete. ("Getting at the History" 81)

Literary scholarship, also slow to respond to changing public perception, may be catching up with other disciplines in this regard. Fred Hobson, for example, has called for more critical attention to what is now happening in southern letters, that is, the emergence of writers from nonaristocratic or middle-class origins:

If one subscribes to the evolutionary theory of fiction . . . what is happening is simply an expansion of the franchise, part of the centuries-old progress in Western literature from a writing by and principally about the privileged—though occasionally *about* lower classes, comically rendered—to a literature by, and treating seriously, the common people. (23)

Contending that critics have not yet devoted enough attention to this trend, Hobson offers the possibility that "class—now that race and gender are being addressed—will be the next enlivening issue in the consideration of southern letters" (20)

If this is currently occurring, and the signs are that it is, it would appear to be because the older elitist sensibility of both critic and writer—the dominant force in southern literature from its beginnings into the 1950s—is now exhausted, anchored as it was in a caste system in which land-ownership gave the aristocracy not only its power but its sense of values. As late as 1982, Andrew Lytle, seeking to defend the validity of the old Agrarian position on this aspect of southern life and literature, could declare that "a southerner would know you would have to have property, something to lose so you would be careful how you would vote and protect yourself. . . . And that is gone, that is gone" (qtd. in Havard and Sullivan 176).

This concept, however, had actually been refuted by southerners long before the Agrarians sought to revive it. As has been noted, post-Civil War writers had tried to usher in a more democratic spirit by pointing to the unrealized potential of the landless "poor white." And although their ideas have been somewhat overshadowed by modern writers such as Faulkner and Welty—who were more influenced, it would seem, by negative antebellum attitudes—their attempts to create understanding of, and sympathy for, disadvantaged southern whites did not die completely, but were actually furthered, during that same modern period, by writers such as Warren and Arnow—whose restructuring of the "redneck" image to include more positive aspects has paved the way for today's genuine attempts at understanding.

# 19

## Robert Penn Warren:
## The Dispossessed as Southerner

Robert Penn Warren is not the artist that Faulkner is, nor do his characters leap from the page as do O'Connor's. But what strikes the reader about Warren is his capacity for analysis and a desire for understanding. Not the least of what Warren came to understand, in ways Faulkner and O'Connor did not, was the psychological makeup and motivation of poverty-striken rural white citizens of the South. This understanding seems to have come from his readings into what he called "the testimony of sociologists and historians," which allowed him a historical perspective and insight into the contemporary milieu of despair and hopelessness of disadvantaged rural whites (Millichap 98).

Warren's readiness to understand and therefore sympathize with the dispossessed came early. As he himself recalls in his essay "All the King's Men: The Matrix of Experience," he first traveled from his native Kentucky to the deep south of Louisiana State University not knowing what to expect. He soon found, however, that the students there were much "like students everywhere in the country in the big state universities." The ones who engaged his most immediate sympathy, however, were the few rural students from the outlying parishes who occasionally, despite economic, social, and psychological obstacles, made it to that campus but were still discouraged about their ability to learn. Recalling that experience later, he expressed his sympathy with those students as well as an antipathy for the attitudes of the upper and middle classes:

Among the students there sometimes appeared . . . that awkward boy from the depth of the 'Cajun' country or from some scrabblefarm in north Louisiana, with burning ambition and frightening energy and a thirst for learning; and his presence there, you reminded yourself . . .

was due to Huey [Long] and to Huey alone. For the "better element" had done next to nothing in fifty years to get that boy out of the grim despair of his ignorance. (*Selected Essays* 78)

In that same essay, Warren writes of picking up a hitchhiker on his initial trip to Baton Rouge, revealing again his willingness to understand the historical and psychological reasons behind the outward appearance and behavior of the disadvantaged white. Also revealed here is Warren's tendency to dignify rather than belittle rural people:

Along the way I picked up a hitchhiker—a country man, the kind you call a redneck or a wool-hat, aging, aimless, nondescript, beat up by life and hard times and bad luck, clearly tooth-broke and probably gut-shot, standing beside the road in an attitude that spoke of infinite patience and considerable fortitude, holding a parcel in his hand, wrapped in old newspaper and tied with binder twine, waiting for some car to come along. He was, though at the moment I did not sense it, a mythological figure . . . the god on the battlement . . . a voice, a portent, and a natural force like the Mississippi River getting set to bust a levee. (76)

In this passage, not only is Warren working out his sense of the almost mythological force behind the huge popularity of Huey Long, but he is seeing the hitchhiker, not as an aberration or perversion of the natural order—as most southern writers from William Byrd on have seen him—but as a human being closer to nature than his more prosperous counterpart.

Paul West defined Warren's theme in *All the King's Men* as "man earthbound, earthheld, not one with nature but licensed by nature and obliged, always, to subject his aspirations . . . to his sense of being indivisible from an organic whole he has not himself created" (31). If this is so, and the whole of Warren's work points to its validity, then it is also true that in the modern world where most people live fragmented lives, Warren believed that the most "authentic" people were dispossessed whites, and he illustrates this in his characterizations of Jeff York in "The Patented Gate and the Mean Hamburger," Willie Proudfit in *Night Rider,* and Ashby Wyndam in *At Heaven's* Gate—all of whom hark back to a more idyllic time in the history of the South before progress and "newfangledness" intruded on the natural world and diminished the quality of life.

When Warren wrote his essay "The Briar Patch" for the 1930 Agrarian tract *I'll Take My Stand,* he assumed attitudes about African-Americans he was to later regret and alter, but he was well in advance of his contemporaries in discerning the psychological motivations of the "poor white" who he felt "to be just as much the victim of the slave system as the Negro" and who in an "inarticulate fashion . . . realizes this fact and from it comes much of the individual violence, such as lynching" (258-60).

For this reason Warren joined the other Agrarians in their denunciation of progress, feeling that "unchecked industrialism" would cause the poor of both races to engage in "cutthroat competition" for jobs. In such a desperate situation, the white, already smarting under a legacy of unjust treatment, would, he felt, resort to yet more violence.

But even here, Warren held out hope. The "poor white," he wrote in that 1930 essay, can be educated from fear into a cooperation with blacks and eventually work side by side with them harmoniously. It is in his belief that the poor of both races are capable of being educated that Warren parts company with his fellow Agrarians (258-60).

"As a border state southerner," James H. Justus writes, Warren "would be as prepared as his fellow Agrarians to flinch from the commercial spirit of progress . . . but he would never quite find alternatives to it in a refashioned image of an arcadian south" (321). One reason for this is that at the same time the Agrarians elevated the land-owning "yeoman" farmer to almost mythical stature, they relegated the "poor white" without land to the status of outsider and misfit. Warren, on the other hand, saw the "poor white" closer to being natural than were his more sophisticated urban counterparts. Thus his decline to a dispossessed status in contemporary society became for Warren a tragedy that genuinely engaged his sympathy.

That sympathy is evident in several of Warren's short stories. The nine-year-old narrator of "Blackberry Winter," for example, thinks of "a squatter [who] lived up in the hills" as "poor white trash." But when he tells his father about the squatter losing a cow in the flood and calls the squatter "Milt Alley," his father corrects him: "You say 'Mr. Alley.'"

This "social parallelism," as Joseph R. Millichap terms it (20-21), is underscored later when a Civil War veteran tries to save a poor white boy embarrassment when the boy expresses a desire to eat a drowned cow. "Live long enough," the veteran says, "and a man will settle for what he can git." It is further significant that this episode is handled not as grotesque humor but in a genuinely sympathetic and understanding manner.

In "The Patented Gate and the Mean Hamburger," Warren's narrator gives the reader historical perspective on the plight of the dispossessed rural whites:

> They were croppers. . . . They were the great-great-great grandsons of men who, half woodsmen and half farmers, had been shoved into the sand hills, into the limestone hills, into the barrens, two hundred, two hundred and fifty years before and had learned there the way to grabble a life out of the sand and the stone. . . . But there was a curse on them. . . . [Yet their] eyes are alive. . . . They have endured and they will endure in their silence and wisdom. (121-22)

This and similar passages in which Warren brings to his writing what he has learned from his extensive reading reveal the truth of Paul West's statement that Warren always does his "homework" (8). It is because of his willingness to educate himself, without the blinders of prejudice that have kept so many others from learning historical truths, that Warren is able to give his disadvantaged white characters the innate intelligence denied them by so many other writers. He also does not superficially lay the blame for their impoverished situation on their being "shiftless and lazy." Instead, he cites historical factors that have acted upon them to bring them to their present misery. This willingness to incorporate sociological studies into his thinking and his writing separates him from his fellow Agrarians, several of whom denounced such studies as socialistic.

Fortunately, Warren had no such problem. On the contrary, he has described the pleasure he derived from such studies, one instance being his research for the characterization of Jeff York in "The Patented Gate." "I saw that man," he writes, "in the perspective of history and in the perspective of a great social shift in our time." This realization caused Warren to feel "a surge of emotion. . . . I saw how great had been the odds against him. I saw how he had struggled to escape the doom of his luckless class and kind" (qtd. in Millichap 98).

"The Patented Gate and the Mean Hamburger" is the story of Jeff York, one of the few who has supposedly "broken the curse" of the sharecropper to become a successful farmer, acquiring a place in society denied the others, although he still identifies with his humble origins and feels comfortable only in the company of his sharecropper friends. With his newly found success, however, he is able to buy a gate which he places at the entrance to his farm, a "seal Jeff York had put on all the years of sweat and rejection." It is from this gate that he eventually hangs himself.

Jeff York is defeated for several reasons. First, his wife tries to push him into a commercial endeavor far removed from his natural affinity with the land; second, he sells his land, which, as Warren states elsewhere, "is, literally, life and death" to him but merely "a sort of toy" for the man who buys it (qtd. in Millichap 98).

But most of all we sense that York, borne down by the burden of his history—and the history of his ancestors—could not, in the end, truly break the "curse" that Warren tells us is on all sharecroppers. Even in success, he is drawn back to the impoverished "croppers" he has struggled so hard to rise above. And in no one else's company, including his wife's, does he feel comfortable. Faulkner gives the same sense of tragic irony to Sutpen, who also cannot overcome his "poor white" past.

Warren is less successful in his treatment of Willie Proudfit in *Night Rider* (1939), for that character appears as the central figure of a story within the story, seemingly thrown in to present Warren's theme of self-realization. Nevertheless, as Justus notes, Proudfit is the only character in an otherwise nihilistic novel who "can be said to have passed from a negative state of violence and confusion to a positive state of self-knowledge" (162), indicating once more Warren's predilection to give knowledge and true wisdom to characters from the lowest strata of society. Proudfit, however, is not a fully realized character and remains only a mechanical symbol of Warren's theme.

An even less successful characterization is that of Ashby Wyndam in *At Heaven's Gate* (1943) who is also "poor white" and who also comes to self-awareness, but who, as Justus has noted, is "so unremittingly radical and fundamentalist" that he negates his role as "a model of growth for others." But there is another "poor white" in this novel, the protagonist's father, who takes his son in hand, offering in the words of Justus, "the possibility of regeneration" that Warren denies the other middle-class characters (162-63).

A more successful characterization of a rural character is that of Willie Stark in *All the King's Men* (1946). Willie is not, strictly speaking, poor, but his family has struggled long and hard to earn a living from the land. Moreover, Willie has true sympathy for his poverty-stricken neighbors. There is one part of him, as Louis D. Rubin notes, that has strong affinities with the Snopses, namely his "unabashed expediency and pragmatic effectiveness" as well as his reliance on "force and cunning." But, as Rubin further notes, there is a "striking difference. . . . Willie is no crass material-ist" but "possesses stature, purpose, ideals," qualities notably absent in Faulkner's Snopes clan (*Faraway* 119-20, 124). And despite having succumbed to Snopesian traits, which in turn bring about his own downfall, Willie remains to the end, a human being. If he is a Snopes in any sense, he is, to use Thomas Daniel Young's term, a "humanized" Snopes (82).

In *Flood* (1963), Warren gives his main character, Brad Tol-liver, a "redneck" background in that his father is "a trueborn muskrat skinner" who emerges from the west Tennessee swamps "bar' foot and one gallus" and proceeds, Snopes fashion, to take over the town of Fiddlersburg in an unscrupulous fashion, fore-close on its most prominent citizen, old Doc Fiddler, and take pos-session of the Fiddler mansion.

All of this leads, of course, to the conclusion that Warren, by now, may well have read Faulkner's Snopes trilogy, but he nonetheless gives to his character the realistic capacity of feeling uncomfortable in his newly acquired status, which leads him to periodically go back to the place of his origins and to "disappear into the swamp and weep" (118-19). One day, in a gesture of mis-trust and resentment of civilization, the old man, reminiscent of Faulkner's Ab Snopes, proceeds to burn books from the Fiddler library, tearing pages out one by one and throwing them into the fire. In this scene Brad, as a young boy, assumes the role of the sensitive and ultimately rebellious Sarty, snatching a book from his father's hands and another from the fire despite the fact that his father strikes four blows to his head, the last rendering him unable to get up from the floor (116-17). Warren further parallels the old man with Ab Snopes in making him a "bushwhacker" and, according to Brad, desirous of acquiring the Fiddler mansion "so he could track in swamp mud or cow dung" (53).

The figure of his father haunts Brad, who is equally uncom-fortable in society. In the words of his sister, he "prides himself on not being an aristocrat" and half in pride, half in disdain, he describes himself as a "descendent of a long line of Choctaw-screwing, jug walloping, muscrat-skinners from the deep swamps," preferring "river-rat types" to polite society, taking as his best friend an illiterate "swamp rat" and ex-bushwhacker named Frog-Eye, whom he considers the "only free man left" (51, 115).

Warren adds another valid touch to Brad by making him ashamed of his background, a shame that strikes him only when he leaves Fiddlersburg for prep school where he is made to feel poor, a feeling that pursues him all of his life, causing him to be continually discontented and on the edge of anger, especially against those, including his wife, who cause him to feel ashamed of feeling poor. His anger reaches a peak when he commits sexual violence against his wife and then the blind woman Leontine, both of whom are described as excessively fair-skinned, in contrast to his dark-skinned father (181-82, 275, 206).

Brad's identity with his father's outsider status also causes him to denounce the South. Coming upon the Confederate monument that stands in the center of Fiddlersburg, he calls it "Johnny Reb" and heaps ridicule upon it:

He is all that makes Fiddlersburg southern. He is all that gives us the dignity of our defects. He is all that makes paranoid violence into philosophic virtue. Take him away and Fiddlersburg wouldn't be anything but a wore-out bunch of rednecks and reformed swamp rats that had crawled out on dry land, and the dry land nothing but a few acres of worthless real estate. Take Johnny Reb away and . . . Fiddlersburg would be just like Iowa. (256)

In this passage, Warren's protagonist brings together W.J. Cash's thesis that the southern aristocracy had few claims to anything but a plebeian past, with the arguments of such recent writers as Walker Percy and Richard Ford who question whether the South is truly any different from the rest of the country and who wish to be considered American and not southern writers. As for the Old South plantation myth, Warren's protagonist denounces it as "lies" (256).

And yet Brad feels drawn to Fiddlersburg and returns to it after living in New York City and Hollywood because it's the only place where he has not been made to feel ashamed of his background. This would at first appear to strike a false note and to reveal limitations to Warren's understanding of class psychology, for it is primarily fellow townspeople who make the dispossessed most aware of their unequal status. But then, Brad is not, strictly speaking, economically lower class, since his father owns most of the town. In fact, his alienation is due to his father's "redneck" background, traits of which he feels he has inherited, and the shame of which he cannot shed. In removing Brad a generation away from poverty but inheriting a sense of inferiority because of his ancestors, Warren has hit on a theme that transcends economics and extends lower-class alienation to many southerners who are not, in fact, lower-class at all, but who do not feel far enough removed from that condition to have cast aside many of the feelings that the truly disadvantaged have.

Thus in Brad Tolliver, Warren has captured the dilemma of those southerners who suspect that their progenitors may well have been the equivalent of "swamp rats." This feeling is compounded by the post-Civil War sense of defeat and impoverishment most southerners felt and which has taken a century to overcome. It is this affinity with poverty, past and present, that causes southerners to make fun of, even scorn, the "redneck," while applying that term, though half in jest, to themselves. This dilemma is complicated by the reality of disintegrating southern traditions and the sameness of life in both North and South. Warren suggests a solution to the paradox through Brad Tolliver who finally transcends both Fiddlersburg and the South by concluding that, in the end, "there is no country but the heart."

Warren further pursues this theme in *A Place to Come To* (1977) whose protagonist Jed Tewksbury tries throughout to psychologically overcome his southern poverty background. "We were poor," he tells a fellow professor, "dirt poor," and he describes the house he grew up in as an "about-to-fall-down weatherboard house, long since paintless and with cardboard stuck behind a broken windowpane and one thread of poverty smoke unspooling forever upward from the kitchen chimney" (5).

Jed's father, whom Warren unfortunately treats as a comic figure, comes off as a stereotype, though not strictly of the "redneck," but rather of a combination of that and an incongruously aristocratic defender of the Lost Cause. He is, according to Tewksbury, a "feckless, vanity-bit dreamer" who marries into a landholding family, acquires a substantial farm, which he allows to "dwindle" to forty acres "and then, by way of a mortgage, to thirty" (13).

He spends much of his time getting drunk and neglecting the farm. At one point he buys a sword at an auction for fifty cents, which he claims is a "confederate saber his old grandad had used to fight Yankees." In his drunken stupor—which seems his con-

stant state—he brandishes the "rusty old blade" in imaginary battles with Union troops until he collapses on the hearth and is
hauled off to bed by his wife (2).

His drunkenness eventually causes his death when one day
he halts his wagon on the road, stands up and proceeds "to piss
on the hind quarters of a span of mules," then pitch "forward on
his head, still hanging on to his dong," after which the wagon
rolls over his neck. His "dong," a neighbor points out, "is about
all Buck Tewksbury had left to hang on to" (1, 4).

This episode seems oddly out of place in the novel as the
slapstick tone of it contrasts so starkly with the seriousness of the
novel as a whole. Unfortunately, Warren's protagonist brings up
this episode again and again, evidently to reinforce the truth of
the neighbor's comment.

Tewksbury's mother, who comes from a more prosperous
family, descends into poverty along with her husband but steadfastly denies the label of "pore white trash" her son insists on calling her. "She must have been very good-looking in her girlhood,"
he says, "but as is usual among pore white trash . . . whatever
beauty she had has long since been ravaged" (83). After her husband's death, determined that "she was not born white trash and
didn't aim to die that way," she sells the house and thirty acres,
moves to town, and goes to work in a canning factory. But her life
quickly descends into monotonous drudgery as she goes "to and
from the cannery, to and from the cookstove and bed" (13-14).

Again unfortunately, Tewksbury moves from clinical observation of his mother to grotesque comedy in an episode that
recalls Faulkner's Anse Bundren's preoccupation with getting
false teeth. She writes to her son in Chicago, "I did not want you
to see me old and ugly and one tooth gone in front. Gonna put
back a aritfisil one soon as I can pay cash." Later she sends him a
photo taken at a studio "with mouth pulled back in a comic-strip,
lip-splitting grin and forefinger dramatically pointing to a fine
prominent brilliantly white incisor" (275).

The problem with this episode is that it is hard to imagine a
poverty-striken old woman finally scraping up enough money for
a tooth and a photo session, then turning her once-in-a-lifetime
portrait into a grotesque comic image—especially as she did not
want her son to see her looking "old and ugly." But here again, as
with the episodes involving the father, Warren allows his protagonist-narrator to fall from the extreme seriousness of one who has
experienced the indignities of poverty to a tone reminiscent of the

Southwest humorists whose perspective on their subjects was always condescending.

It is the same incongruous combination we see in Caldwell, of course—the sympathetic, textbook explanations of the causes and effects of poverty juxtaposed to depictions of the poor as grotesque buffoons. But somehow Caldwell pulls it off better, principally because he seems more at home with low-comedy than does Warren.

But when Warren moves away from attempts at humor, his writing reflects a knowledge of the reality of poverty. This is evident in Tewksbury's rejection of the high school girl Rozelle who, he feels, only wishes to exploit his "lowly social condition" and "stoop to the peasant boy" (48). It is also apparent in his "disgust and anger" at the middle-class professional people he meets at parties in Nashville where he experiences a "great wave of despair, of lostness" from his unsuccessful attempts to bridge their world. He realizes his background prevents him from ever feeling a part of their lives and envies one party-goer who "was programmed in a hell of a lot different way from me." Unable to find in Nashville a place where he can fit in, he despairs of ever touching "native earth" (196, 200).

The people at the parties contrast sharply with the people he has grown up with in Dugtown. Those he describes as "real, existing in flesh and blood, struggling with their lives, full of affliction, weakness, rage, and vice, but somehow capable of love and courage, sustained by hope and irony." But he also realizes that his earlier sense of "place" in his hometown is also lost to him and he accepts his mother's advice that he not move back because there "ain't nothing here for you" (7, 26).

Tewksbury's anger, frustration, and despair, however, are as much the result of his being a southerner as of having been poor as a child, experiences that to Warren are intertwined. "Hating the south," Tewksbury says at one point, "I had to flee it, and ever afterwards blamed my solitude on that fact." He even feels that the tone of his academic writings stems "from some sense of outrage at the world whose language and dialect I had been now and then contemptuously echoing, and an indefinable sense of outrage at myself." His self-contempt is aggravated, moreover, when he succumbs to his Chicago colleagues' stereotype of him as a southern "redneck" and begins to "play the role of southerner to the hilt." Part of this is telling tall tales in an exaggerated "hillbilly" accent and language (295, 6, 17).[1]

The novel, however, has problems, not the least of which is the sentimental ending in which Tewsbury recaptures his sense of "a place to come to" through exposure to "innocent" and "good" characters like his mother's new husband, Park, and Mrs. McInnis, who assures Tewksbury that his mother's portrait is not grotesque at all but is rather the picture of a woman with "guts." Through these influences, Tewksbury recaptures what a colleague refers to as his *"sancta simplicitas"* (327, 339).

A more serious problem is Tewksbury's picturing of his parents as grotesque comic figures. Any person who rises out of poverty to become a member of the professional class might authentically feel ashamed of his parents, as does Brad Tolliver in *Flood*, but it is hard to imagine such a person making constant fun of them. A few instances of this might have worked to some extent had Warren confined them to Tewksbury's entertainment of his colleagues at parties, playing, the "stage southerner." But Warren, for the most part, includes them in the narration directed toward the reader. For example, the mother's making a clown of herself in the portrait is an actual event in the story, as is the father's death scene.

Another problem—perhaps more of a gaff, really—is Tewksbury's straying from authenticated historical facts about disadvantaged whites in the South to an off-hand comment about "the rise of the rednecks" (194). The fictional ascent to power by the poorest of the poor was first promoted by pre-Civil War aristocrats and their allies, the Southwest humorists, who sought to counter the extension of the vote to the "common man" during the Jackson era. The concept, which was given further literary life by Faulkner during a later period of political unrest, has been shown to be historically false (Jehler 141).

Nonetheless, this novel, however problematic, is Warren's effort to understand and illustrate a much-neglected theme—the anger, frustration, and low self-image of those with a poverty background—and to show how this relates to southerners in general. Justus has rightly noted that one of Warren's themes is "the painful struggle for self-knowledge" in a world of "social disorder and personal inauthenticity" (1). Warren's importance lies at least partly in that he saw so clearly that this struggle was most painfully felt by the southern "rednecks."

# 20

## Harriette Arnow:
## The Dispossessed as Self-Reliant Woman

The characters Harriette Arnow is chiefly interested in are those inhabitants of the mountains of eastern Kentucky who, seemingly forgotten by time, found themselves having to make a choice, from the 1920s onward, of either remaining in the hills in poverty or moving to the industrialized urban areas of the North where they faced an uncertain future.

Her first insight into these people's lives came about when she, as a novice eighteen-year-old from a relatively prosperous mountain area, was given the assignment to teach in a one-room school in an isolated, impoverished valley that lay, as she put it, "in the rows and rows of hills to the east . . . where few people whom I knew had ever visited." What she encountered there was, as she wrote in an introduction to the 1964 reissue of her novel *Mountain Path*, a shock to her heretofore protected middle-class sensibility:

Life in the hills was on the whole worse than it had been for decades. The big timber was gone, the oil, and the soil washed from the hillsides and ridge tops; game was scarce. There was little left but scrub timber, worn out soil, and people. . . . The average school was a one room frame building . . . no toilets of any kind, water from the closest spring . . . and almost no help from the State of Kentucky. Education was on the whole considered a local problem. (v-vii)

The situation was aggravated, she continues, by the fact that there were no roads for the farmers to take to market their crops and livestock: "All the sources of petty cash open to families such as my own around Burnside—the sale of eggs and poultry, dairy products, vegetables, the shipping of cream—were not to be found in the roadless, marketless hill community" (ix).

Another aspect of hill life that surprised Arnow, who had been given the stereotypical version of hostile mountaineers, was their hospitality:

I was able to join in the life of the people. They invited me. Often we walked or rode muleback together to church. I remember molasses stiroffs and music parties and a rousing charivari. There were no post-boxes, so we would go around to the post office to get the mail. Other times I went with the landlady across the Cumberland to another store. (qtd. in Eckley 34)

Arnow was so impressed by these people that she took it as her life's work to defend them against the kind of prejudice she encountered when she moved to Detroit during the Second World War and heard them referred to as "rednecks and ridgerunners, and worse still, hillbillies and snakes." There, she writes, "I was often at odds with people who said hill children were stupid because they were troubled by the traffic, or because they sometimes missed school to go home to the mountains. I knew better" (qtd. in Flynn 242, 253).

Arnow set out not only to correct such bigoted attitudes but to expose as well the equally condescending assumption by well-meaning people that they can empathize with the poor because they "know" them. She dramatizes the falsity of both ways of thinking, beginning with her first published story, "The Washer-woman's Day," accepted by Robert Penn Warren for the *Southern Review in* 1936.

That story is told from the perspective of Jane, a nine- or ten-year-old girl, who learns of the death of a woman named Clarie Bolin who has been making her living by cleaning houses and washing clothes for the middle-class citizens of the town, including Jane's mother, whose chief concern is that she will now have to resort to hiring "a nigger from Canetown" to do the work. Clarie has died of pneumonia as a result of going barefoot while scubbing a prominent citizen's kitchen floor, a practice Jane's mother attributes to "the old fool" wishing to save her new shoes.

The plot involves an encounter between Jane and the washer-woman's surviving daughter that jolts her out of the paternalistic assumptions about "poor white trash" that she has inherited from her family and friends, assumptions that solidify her mother and grandmother in their smugness, but do nothing to explain the actual behavior of those people. She learns that, despite all she has believed before, she does not know them at all.

The encounter takes place at Clarie's funeral, which has been paid for by the Ladies Aid Society. Jane and her friend sit in the back row observing Clarie's daughter, who sits up front in an ill-fitting coat given her by one of the ladies. She holds in her lap a baby we are led to believe has been fathered by the girl's employer. After the service, several of the ladies give her six of the roses they have purchased for the funeral, keeping the remainder for the sewing circle the following day.

Jane's jolt into a disquieting view of the class structure comes about when the daughter doesn't act as she and the other people think she should. First, she has brought the baby to the funeral, which the others take as an affront. Second, she doesn't cry at the sermon which Jane feels is "wonderful" but which is, in fact, condescending. Third, she doesn't respond with "so much as a thank-you" for the gift of flowers. Finally, when she feels she is safely away from the others, she tramples the flowers into the mud.

The basic lesson Jane learns is that there is anger among these people that she wasn't aware of. This she notices first when she looks into the coffin and wonders why "the dead woman looked the way she did with her teeth clamped tight together and her thin blue lips drawn back a little ways . . . as if she had just come back from a long fight and had lost the fight" (525). In addition, instead of cooperating with the paternalistic system, which Jane takes to be benevolent, the daughter seems instead to angrily resent it.

But the most telling thing for Jane is the daughter's seeming refusal to cry during the entire affair. The act of crying, as well as a show of gratitude to the ladies, would complete the neat cycle of events set up by the ladies in their "benevolence" and justify the whole system of paternalism they have set in motion. "She's not even crying," Jane tells her friend after the sermon. "She looked mad." This realization is disturbing to Jane. "I . . . didn't want to whisper anymore," she says. "It was no longer fun" (524).

Disquieted by this revelation, Jane continues to watch "to see how she would manage" as the coffin is taken out of the church, but the girl simply lays "the baby and the roses on the seat and climbed in" the buggy, as stoic in appearance as she had been inside the church. Later at the cemetery, Jane's friend whispers that Laurie Mae "means to put the roses on the grave," but Jane notes that she "didn't do that." Still later the two approach the girl with a comment that the flowers had cost three dollars, thinking "she would be pleased to know the Ladies Aid had spent so much," but Laurie Mae is not impressed; she simply responds, "I know. It's a lot of money," her voice sounding "full of something else. We didn't know what it was" (527).

Still Jane is not satisfied, and when her friend leaves the cemetery, she hides behind the concrete pillars of the gate and waits. "I wanted to see Laurie Mae," she says. "I thought that now she was alone she might cry. I wanted to see her cry." But still Laurie Mae does not behave according to Jane's scenario. Instead she throws the roses into the "yellow mud of the road," pushing them with her foot and raking mud over them, after which she picks up her baby and leaves (527).

Jane is not fully cognizant of the ramifications of her new awareness, for after all, she is a young girl. But we do know she will not return to her former assurance, nor will she look upon her peers in the community in the same way. For she is forever separated from them in her new and disquieting knowledge.

Arnow carries the theme further in her semiautobiographical novel *Mountain Path* (1936), in which Louisa Sheridan, fresh from the University of Kentucky, takes her first teaching job in a remote mountain region called Canebrake, not unlike the mountain area where Arnow herself first taught. Arnow, however, creates in Louisa innocence beyond her own by giving her no previous rural experience at all, let alone in "a kind a lost like place" where she is forced to cope with a way of life so primitive she had not been aware that it existed. Confirmed in her superiority to such people, she vows nonetheless to stay with the job until she has made enough money to continue her schooling, returning at that point to "people of her own kind" (12).

As the novel progresses, however, Louisa slowly emerges from her smugness to at least some awareness of the hill folk's humanity. In the process, she learns a more natural sense of things, including a knowledge of time measured by the sun and the seasons and an understanding and acceptance of motivational drives such as revenge that she would have before condemned out of hand. She also learns very soon to become "irked" by the attitudes of the "sophisticated" people of Lexington who would not concede that "the beings she worked with were people" (58, 53). But she also wavers throughout the novel between being a bystander and a participant to such an extent that neither she nor the reader can be sure of how she will feel in the future.

That may, however, be the point. Life is not a process in which we learn certain truths and never waiver from them. Least of all should we expect someone as young, and as previously innocent, as Louisa to have come to a final understanding that will govern her life forever.

Nevertheless, we can say that Louisa has been changed by her experience and that she has learned enough so that she will not return to her former smug sense of superiority. She need not become one of "them" to have acquired tolerance. If she has learned in the brief time she is there to respect a way of life and a people she cannot truly know, then perhaps that is enough.

Arnow's next novel, *Hunter's Horn* (1949), is less successful, principally because here the author seems to be making the mistake of her earlier protagonists in assuming she knows disadvantaged whites to the extent that she can go from the limited point of view of the novice schoolteacher in *Mountain Path* to an omniscience that allows her to enter the minds of not only the hill woman, which she comes close to knowing, but also a hill man, which she does not. Abandoning the method of the earlier novel where she renders the male characters through dialogue and action only—a method she uses once more in *The Dollmaker*—in *Hunter's Horn* she attempts to capture the innermost thoughts of her main character, Nunnely Balew, and in the process, creates more stereotype than individual, which is unfortunate since her object is obviously to humanize him.

Nunnely is the owner of a "place at the mouth of Little Smokey Creek on the big South Fork of the Cumberland" that has "come down from his great-great-grandfather." The land, once fertile, has "gone pretty much to brush and gullies," largely through the neglect of a former owner who had bought the land from Nunn's grandfather. Nunn, in the meantime, has gone off to the coal fields to work and save money to buy back the land, which he does, but too late to restore it to its original condition. Nunn, more hunter than farmer, proceeds to neglect the few acres of good land left in favor of searching relentlessly for a notorious fox called King Devil that has destroyed much livestock and has run many a hound to his death. In the end, the fox is killed by two pedigree hounds that Nunn has purchased and fed at the expense of his family, who go without proper food and clothing for the duration of the novel.

Nunn does have his good points, however. He is good-natured and loves his children. But his constant wavering between guilt at having neglected his family and surrendering to his obsession to hunt the fox causes the reader to grow more than a little impatient with him, even though Arnow herself has expressed a fondness for him, believing him to be "a symbol of the good and bad in Appalachian people, damned by his stoicism and saved by his guilt" (qtd. in Flynn 256). He seems, in addition, to represent the pioneer-hunter in a world that no longer values hunting as a principal occupation.

His wife, Milly, fares better. She is the one who holds the family together, despite the odds. Moreover, she is self-sufficient, even delivering her own child in the woods in a scene that abounds in authenticity in a way the scenes with Nunn do not, simply because the in-depth thoughts of the woman as she goes through labor pains have a far greater ring of truth than do Nunn's deliberations as to whether he should have a drink or shoot the fox.

The novel does, however, carry the mountain people further into the present time than does *Mountain Path*, for here Arnow deals with effects on the lives of her characters of farm machinery, gravel roads, and Depression era government programs. Here again she does not take sides in the conflict between progress and the past, as did others of her time, including advocates of the New South on the one hand and the Agrarians on the other. She simply presents characters, some of whom cooperate with the new ways of doing things and others who do not. Nunnely Balew seems, in the end, to be among the former, selling his dogs, buying farm machinery, and making plans for planting tobacco and living "a righteous life; no more drinken an acrousen around" (405).

The novel does not end happily, however, in that Nunn's teenage daughter, who has become pregnant by a man she doesn't want to marry and who has gone off to live in Cincinnati, is forced by Nunn to save the family reputation by going to live with the man's parents even though he is aware she will spend the rest of her days in back-breaking toil, caring for the couple as they grow old. This she will do instead of going off to high school and eventually marrying her college-bound friend that she is much fonder of than she is the father of the child. Nunn here reverts to the old values, which hold that having a "bastard" in the house is disgraceful. His recalcitrance illustrates that it is easier to adapt to new methods of farming than it is to let go of long-held notions of morality, no matter the consequences. In this, Arnow proves herself a realist and not a romantic.

Gertie Nevels, the protagonist of *The Dollmaker* (1954) is a farm woman from the same area as Nunnely Balew. In fact, she and her husband sharecrop on land belonging to Nunn's uncle, John, from whom she plans to buy acreage when she has saved up enough money. Gertie is a self-sufficient, hard-working woman, content to live in the mountains for the rest of her life. The problem arises when her husband Clovis, who is better at tinkering with machinery than he is at farming, drives to Cincinnati at the outbreak of World War II to take an army physical. When the army doesn't want him, he drives up to Detroit, gets a job in a defense plant, and sends for Gertie and the children.

Although extremely reluctant to go—she has finally acquired enough money to buy the land she has desired for so long—Gertie dutifully goes by train to Detroit where she and her family are forced to live in a cramped government housing project that contrasts sharply with the open spaces of their mountain home. In addition, they are subjected to prejudice when the resentful urban-dwellers make fun of them, calling them "hillbillies" and ridiculing them for, among other things, the way they talk and their lack of experience in dealing with store clerks.

Gertie is the dollmaker of the title. Having learned to whittle at a young age and possessing a great amount of artistic talent, she carves beautiful objects from wood she gathers from the timber around the house. When she goes to Detroit she takes along a block of cherry wood that she is attempting to carve into the figure of Christ. She has difficulty in finishing it because she can't envision a face for it. The block remains untouched in the apartment in Detroit for the greater part of the novel until she finally has it split so that she can carve figures from the chunks to sell to a woman who wants them for her church bazaar. There is also a great deal of promise of further markets for her hand-carved dolls.

Gertie's initial problem in finding a face for her Christ figure is that she envisions not an angry Christ, as her mother would have it, but rather "a laughing Christ uncrowned by thorns and with the scars of the nail holes in his hands all healed away; a Christ who had loved people, had liked to mingle with them and laugh and sing," a Christ attuned to forgiveness and tolerance instead of vengeance (54).

This image she loses in the harsh streets of Detroit where she and her family are mocked and ridiculed, in much the way that Christ was on the cross. Now, when she carves, which is infrequently, she can only bring from the wood a figure with lowered head and hands outstretched, palms up.

Moreover, when her daughter Cassie is killed by a train, her oldest son runs away to return to Kentucky, her husband becomes increasingly "tired and angry," and she is unable to feed and clothe her family properly or to give them the confidence they need to grapple with modern life. Indeed, when the only advice she can give them is to "adjust" to the circumstances, Gertie comes to feel that she has betrayed them all and to identify with the ultimate betrayer, Judas. "Was she like Judas," she wonders, "foreordained to sin"? (58). She comes to believe that she is and no longer sees a joyous Christ emerging from the block of wood but a penitent Judas. The happy image of Christ is further diminished when she is commissioned by her Catholic neighbors to carve crucifixes that depict a bloodied, suffering Christ instead of the joyous one she had earlier envisioned.

Several things happen to alter Gertie's thinking, however, to bring her out of her self-pity and guilt over betraying her family. One is that she develops close friendships in the neighborhood. Another is her being shamed into growing flowers in a small patch of dirt, becoming so involved in nurturing them that she keeps them alive into a chilly September (409, 473). In one sense they preserve for her the past—the earth she digs to plant them is "dark and rich . . . smelling even more like the clean earth back home," and the flowers themselves remind her of the Sweet Williams on the farm (407, 416). But, in another way, they pull her further into the community as neighbors tell her that the flowers make them feel better about the world, and she gives a bouquet to a "girl-like mother" she encounters (442).

Gertie's forgiveness of herself is evident when Mrs. Anderson asks her, "What would you do if you'd learned you'd raised your children all wrong?" She replies, "I recken if somebody told me that, I'd think bout my youngens like I think now—take credit to my raisen them for the good they've got, and give the devil er what was born into em credit for the bad" (539).

Mrs. Anderson serves another function in Gertie's awakening as well, for she is herself something of an artist, too, telling Gertie she has been living in the housing project wishing she could get out into the countryside to paint, but now that she is leaving, she realizes her subjects should have been the people around her. Her problem had been that she had focused on her family to the exclusion of others. "This alley," she concludes, "could keep a thousand artists busy a thousand years" (431).

Gertie learns to share this view. When a family is evicted from their apartment, she contributes money, although she badly needs it herself. And when a young wife is leaving her abusive husband, telling Gertie by way of goodbye, "I wish you'd been my people," Gertie calls after her, "But, honey, we're kin, close kin" (424-25).

Gertie's sense of kinship with the larger community is dramatized further in her last act in the novel—the splitting of the cherry wood block, which is at once symbolic and practical. Noting that the face now coming out of the wood is not Judas but Christ, and that this time there is "no quarreling, no scolding, no question" (535), she nonetheless takes it to the scrap-lumber man to "quarter" so that she can carve it into figures to sell to the public. She consents to the splitting because she no longer sees Christ as an individual. Instead she sees his face in the people around her. When the man reminds her that she had long sought a face for the figure, she replies, "They was so many would ha done: they's a millions a faces plenty fine enough—for him. . . . Why, some a my neighbors down there in the alley—they would ha done" (549).

It is a theme similar to Steinbeck's in *The Grapes of Wrath*, but distinct from Faulkner's tragic vision of unrelieved guilt over the past and Warren's Calvinistic notion of unredeemable humanity—two themes that have been cited as the dominant ones in southern literature. But perhaps southern literature need not be defined so narrowly. When this happens, Arnow will have a larger place.

# 21

# Conclusion:
# Trends and Possibilities

Prominent southern critics have long lamented the "death" of literature in the last four decades, a lessening of power they contribute to a loss of theme and values. Lewis Simpson, for example, argues that writers such as Faulkner were attempting a "reconstruction of the meaning of the past," but that "the only meaningful covenant for the latter-day writer is one with the self on terms generally defined as existential" ("Discovery" 6). George Core has come to the same conclusion. "We live in a society that has no underlying common myth," he writes, "and so as time goes on each writer is probably going to be more inclined to set sail on the seas of the self" (63).

One way out of this solipsism—and it is the mark not only of southern writers but of writers in general—is to cease trying to make sense of one's own relationship to history in favor of looking outside oneself to record history as it is happening to others. For the southern writer, this involves observing and making sense of the rapidly changing social scene, and not simply lamenting the passing of the old order.

Noting that the Civil War, Reconstruction, and the ensuing racial turmoil have provided material for a vast amount of literature in the past, James Dickey has called the "changing social patterns" of our own time "just as far-reaching" and just as appropriate for treatment in fiction. "That aspect of the southern scene is going to make some great novelist possible," he says, adding that such a writer will probably be "a woman rather than a man" (qtd. in Walsh 108-09).

I'm not sure that Dickey would see Bobbie Ann Mason as that novelist, but she certainly points the way. "I'm not nostalgic for the past," she says, adding, "Times change and I'm interested in writing about what's now. To me, the way the south is changing is very dynamic and full of complexity. There's a certain energy

167

there that I don't notice in other parts of the country. It comes out of an innocent hope of possibility" (qtd. in Wilhelm 37).

Mason, born just outside of Mayfield, Kentucky, is a chronicler of the changes occurring in rural and small-town life among families on the verge of breaking into the mainstream but still considered "trailer park trash" by the "better" elements of society. More often than not, these families are splitting up through divorce or separation, and the children are spreading out all over the nation. This is the overriding theme of her first short-story collection, *Shiloh and Other Stories* (1982).

Her best writing, however, occurs in the last chapter of her latest novel, *Feather Crowns* (1993), in which the main character, Christianna Wheeler, looks back on her long life that began in the late nineteenth century. In the process, she debunks traditions long held sacred by many southerners—religion, the past, the close-knit family, and ties to one's place of origin.

"I lost my faith," she says. "I didn't know it at the time, and I never told anybody, not even James [her husband]. But I believe he lost his faith too, and he never let on to me either." As for the past, "don't ever think we lived in the good old days," she says. In fact, during the early part of their marriage, she had been forced to live with her in-laws, the Wheelers, who "talked past each other and never said what was in their hearts" (451-52). She elaborates:

Back then families were so big, it was boardinghouse reach, where the younguns got trompled underfoot and a man and wife might sleep on a pallet in the same room with an old man off in the corner a-wheezing and a-wallering on a corn-shuck mattress. People had so many chillern, and the chillern didn't move off the way they do now. . . . Nowadays people are happier spread out, with just a few in a house. I'm sure everybody breathes easier. (454)

Christianna denounces memory, held most sacred to Eudora Welty's protagonist in *The Optimist's Daughter*.

I'll tell you something about memory. It's like if you took anxiousness or dread and put it up in front of a mirror. What you'd see would be memory, like it's coming out the other side of an event. An event is always worse before it happens or after it happens. But not at the time it happens. You can get through that, because it carries you along. It's afterward that gets you. (454)

She reinforces the need to live in the present in a positive declaration that closes the novel:

I don't aim to live out my days all hunched up over my memories. I want to watch the sun come up and hear a hen cackle over a new-laid egg and feel a kitten purr. And I want to see a flock of blackbirds whirl over the field, making music. Things like that are absolutely new ever time they happen. (454)

Another writer whose "redneck" female protagonists have this same resilience in the face of often overwhelming odds is Pat Carr, also a resident of Kentucky. Several of Carr's stories contain characters of the same socioeconomic background as those of Mason. Her women also bear a striking resemblance to those of Glasgow and Arnow in the way in which they exhibit strength in adversity. A case in point is the abused wife Amy in the novella *Bluebirds* (1993).

Amy is married to Hugh, a Vietnam veteran who alternates long periods of silence with eruptions into violence. Holding onto an idealized version of her former husband, also a Vietnam vet who had left her for another woman but who is now once more divorced, she invites him for a visit, anticipating his arrival with a vague notion of refurbishing the romance. But when his appearance and manner disappoint her and she discovers that he has no intention of rekindling even a friendship, she resolves to take charge of her own life. This she conveys to Hugh with an admonition that "if you ever lift a hand to me again, I'll leave you flat," a promise that Hugh realizes she is bent on keeping.

Lee Smith, born in Virginia and presently living in North Carolina, also seeks to humanize her lower-class characters. A problem in her writing is that it is often clouded by a preference for using dialect, which slows down the reading, even when one has heard such dialect spoken. For this reason, her most effective novel is the epistolary *Fair and Tender Ladies* (1988), which moves from the dialect of the early pages into standard English as the protagonist, Ivy Rowe, becomes educated. The story describes her life from elementary school, ending as she is nearing death, an old woman who has had many disappointments including the failure of her early promise as a writer. She nonetheless becomes resigned to her long life, reconciling the unhappy moments as part of an overall scheme she has gleaned from readings in Ecclesiastes: "There is a time for every purpose under heaven."

She dies, believing the bad times were always tempered by the good.

Fred Chappell, of North Carolina, is another writer who views "rednecks" as possessing a basic dignity, although, unlike Smith, he does not sentimentalize them. He too is always sympathetic. For example, in the short story "Children of Strikers," he effectively illustrates the constant threat of violence in an Appalachian mining town when two children find the amputated foot of a doll. Another instance is his characterization of the lower-class orphan, Johnson Gibbs, in *I Am One of You Forever* (1985). Gibbs goes to work for the protagonist-narrator's father and becomes the father's best friend as well as a role model for the protagonist. Gibbs's girlfriend and her father, McClain Lee, are also presented sympathetically and nonstereotypically.

Chappell's understanding of the anger of the "redneck" is revealed in the episode of *Brighten the Corner Where You Are* (1989) involving the young protagonist-narrator and the tenant family who work for his father. The father explains to the narrator the injustice of the tenant farming system and how it keeps the tenant "poor forever and . . . breaks his pride. Turns him mean sometimes." He assures his son he isn't talking about the tenant who works for him, but the son knows, because "Hob Farnum was fierce" (103-14).

The story involves the narrator's confrontation with Hob when he unintentionally strikes the tenant's son, a blow the tenant takes as an insult. The resolution comes as the narrator becomes convinced that there must be continual confrontation and physical violence between the classes and he resolves to come out on top in each instance, an ironic ending that illustrates Chappell's statement in a recent interview that "class lines certainly do exist, and it's very hard for justice to prevail equally" in such a situation. He added that justice is for him "a constant theme" (qtd. in Palmer 407).

The beauty of Chappell's characterization of the narrator is that we empathize with him at the same time we see he is making a wrong conclusion. This is partly due to the fact that the wrong conclusion comes when the story evolves into a "tall tale" of sorts and the boy rises to superhuman strength and overpowers the much bigger tenant's son. Nevertheless, it is Chappell's ability to create sympathy for all of his characters that allows the message to come through that violence does not occur because one person is good and the other evil, but rather because of the capacity of one person to misconstrue the intent of another. It is evident in this case that the tenant system, which pits one class against another, is the real villain.

These, of course, are not the only contemporary southern writers worth serious consideration, but simply a few within a small group who have written seriously about disadvantaged whites. The vast majority of emerging southern writers have understandably populated their fiction with predominantly middle-class characters. Thus these few might be said to exemplify a small but not insignificant trend in southern writing, a trend toward picturing "rednecks" more sympathetically, realistically, and in a less stereotypical manner than they have often been presented in the past. If this trend continues, we will all be the better for it.

# Notes

### Chapter 1

1. Bailey points out that one of Owsley's graduate student researchers examined the documents Bailey uses, which were housed in the Tennessee State Library and Archives a few blocks from Owsley's Vanderbilt office, but that Owsley did not use them in *Plain Folks* because they challenged his thesis. Bailey cites other sources to demonstrate that Owsley was something less than objective as a historian. In one such instance, Owsley admits in a letter to being so bitter about attacks on the South that "I feel I am losing my poise as a historian" (qtd. in Bailey 103).

### Chapter 2

1. It might be noted that the same "repair or mend" ethic is at work when present day "rednecks" save old cars or trucks for parts in order to keep one vehicle in running order.

### Chapter 12

1. See Faulkner's friend Phil Stone on the Snopes trilogy, which he dubbed "The Rise of the Rednecks," commenting that "the real revolution in the South was not the race situation but the rise of the redneck, who did not have any of the scruples of the old aristocracy, to places of power and wealth" (qtd. in Blotner, *Faulkner: A Biography* 331, 192).

### Chapter 16

1. In addition to the verbal accolades, McCarthy has won the following awards: an American Academy of Arts and Letters Fellowship (1965), a Rockefeller Grant (1966-68), a Guggenheim Fellowship (1969), a MacArthur Fellowship (1981), the National Book Award (1992), and the National Book Circle Award (1993).

2. Lorenz's conclusion was based on erroneous information. According to Dr. Kenneth Oakley of the British Museum, the deposits near Peking, which Lorenz cited as evidence, actually contain only animal bones. See Ashley Montague, *The Nature of Human Aggression* (New York: Oxford University Press, 1976), 109-10.

## Chapter 19

1. This might possibly be taken as a parody of Warren's pupil and friend, Jesse Stuart, whom Allen Tate accused of presenting "a dramatization of himself as the Hill-billy for New York consumption" (qtd. in Edwin T. Arnold, "The Canonization of Jesse Stuart" 33).

# Works Cited

**Primary Sources**

Arnow, Harriette. *The Dollmaker*. Lexington: UP of Kentucky, 1985.

——. *Hunter's Horn*. Lexington: UP of Kentucky, 1986.

——. *Mountain Path*. Lexington: UP of Kentucky, 1985.

——. "The Washerwoman's Day." *Southern Review* 1 (1936): 522-27.

Byrd, William. *Histories of the Dividing Line Betwixt Virginia and North Carolina*. Intro. Percy G. Adams. New York: Dover, 1967.

Cable, George Washington. *Bonaventure*. New York: Scribner, 1888.

——. *Dr. Sevier*. New York: Scribner, 1925.

Caldwell, Erskine. *American Earth*. New York: Scribner, 1931.

——. *Call It Experience: The Years of Learning How to Write*. New York: Duell, 1951.

——. *God's Little Acre*. New York: Viking, 1934.

——. *A House in the Uplands*. New York: Duell, 1946.

——. *Kneel to the Rising Sun and Other Stories*. New York: Viking, 1935.

——. Preface. *Tobacco Road*. By Caldwell. Savannah: Beehive P, 1974.

——. *Southways*. New York: Viking, 1938.

——. *This Very Earth*. New York: Duell, 1948.

——. *Tobacco Road*. New York: Modern Library, 1932.

——. *Tragic Ground*. New York: Duell, 1944.

——. *Trouble in July*. New York: Duell, 1940.

Carr, Pat. "Bluebirds." *Careless Weeds: Six Texas Novellas*. Ed. Tom Pilkington. Dallas: Southern Methodist UP, 1993.

Chappell, Fred. *Brighten the Corner Where You Are*. New York: St. Martin's, 1989.

——. "Children of Strikers." *Growing Up in the South*. Ed. Suzanne W. Jones. New York: Penguin, 1991.

——. *I Am One of You Forever*. Baton Rouge: Lousiana State UP, 1985.

Chopin, Kate. *Bayou Folk*. 1894. Ridgewood: Gregg, 1967.

——. *A Night in Acadia*. 1897. New York: Garrett, 1968.

Crews, Harry. *Blood and Grits*. New York: Harper, 1979.

——. *A Childhood: The Biography of a Place*. New York, Harper, 1978.

——. *A Feast of Snakes*. New York: Atheneum, 1976.

——. *The Gospel Singer*. New York: Harper, 1968.

Faulkner, William. *Absalom, Absalom!* New York: Random House, 1936.

——. *As I Lay Dying*. New York: Random House, 1930.

——. *Collected Stories*. New York: Random House, 1950.

——. *Go Down Moses*. New York: Random House, 1942.

——. *The Hamlet*. 3rd ed. New York: Random House, 1964.

——. *Light in August*. New York: Random House, 1932.

——. *The Mansion*. New York: Random House, 1959.

——. *The Town*. New York: Random House, 1957.

Glasgow, Ellen. *Barren Ground*. 1925. New York: Hill, 1959.

——. *A Certain Measure: An Interpretation of Prose Fiction*. New York: Harcourt Brace, 1938.

——. *Deliverance*. New York: Doubleday, 1904.

——. *The Miller of the Old Church*. 1911. Garden City: Doubleday, 1913.

——. *The Voice of the People*. New York: Doubleday, 1900.

——. *The Woman Within*. New York: Harcourt Brace, 1954.

Harris, George Washington. *Sut Lovingood*. New York: Grove, 1954.

Harris, Joel Chandler. *Balaam and His Master and Other Sketches and Stories*. Boston: Houghton, 1891.

——. *Free Joe and Other Georgia Sketches*. New York: Scribner, 1887.

——. *Mingo and Other Sketches in Black and White*. Boston: Houghton, 1884.

Hooper, Johnson Jones. *Adventures of Cpt Simon Suggs*. Intro. Manley Wade Wellman. Chapel Hill: U of South Carolina P, 1969.

Longstreet, Augustus B. *Georgia Scenes*. Intro. Richard Harwell. Savannah: Beehive P, 1975.

Mason, Bobbie Ann. *Feather Crowns*. New York: Harper, 1993.

——. *Love Life*. New York: Harper, 1989.

——. *Shiloh and Other Stories*. New York: Harper, 1982.

McCarthy, Cormac. *Child of God*. New York: Random House, 1973.

——. *The Orchard Keeper*. New York: Random House, 1982.

——. *Outer Dark*. New York: Random House, 1968.

——. *Suttree*. New York: Random House, 1986.

O'Connor, Flannery. *The Complete Stories*. New York: Farrar, 1971.

Roberts, Elizabeth Madox. *The Time of Man*. Intro. Robert Penn Warren. New York: Viking, 1963.

Simms, William Gilmore. *Eutaw*. Rev. ed. Chicago: Donohue, Henneberry, 1890.

——. *The Forayers*. New York: Redfield, *1855*.

——. *Richard Hurdis*. Rev. ed. Chicago: Donohue, Henneberry, 1890.

Smith, Lee. *Fair and Tender Ladies*. New York: Putnam's, 1988.

Warren, Robert Penn. *All the King's Men*. New York: Random House, 1946.

——. *At Heaven's Gate*. New York: Random House, 1943.

——. *The Circus in the Attic*. New York: Harcourt Brace, 1948.

——. *Flood.* New York: Random House, 1963.

——. *New and Selected Essays.* New York: Random House, 1989.

——. *Night Rider.* New York: Random House, 1939.

——. *A Place to Come To.* New York: Random House, 1977.

——. *Selected Essays.* New York: Random House, 1958.

Welty, Eudora. *The Collected Stories.* New York: Harcourt Brace, 1980.

——. *Delta Wedding.* New York: Harcourt Brace, 1946.

——. *The Eye of the Story: Selected Essays and Reviews.* New York: Random House, 1977.

——. *Losing Battles.* New York: Random House, 1970.

——. *One Writer's Beginnings.* Cambridge: Harvard UP, 1984.

——. *The Optimist's Daughter.* New York: Random House, 1972.

——. *The Ponder Heart.* San Diego: Harcourt Brace, 1982.

### Secondary Sources

Alderman, Edwin Anderson. "Education in the South." *The South Since Reconstruction.* Ed. Thomas D. Clark. Indianapolis: Bobbs-Merrill, 1970.

Allport, Gordon W. *The Nature of Prejudice.* Reading, Mass.: Addison Wesley, 1954.

Ardrey, Robert. *The Territorial Imperative.* New York: Atheneum, 1966.

Arnold, Edwin T. "The Canonization of Jesse Stuart." *Appalachian Journal* 13 (1985): 28-33.

——, and Dianne C. Luce, eds. *Perspectives on Cormac McCarthy.* Jackson: UP of Mississippi, 1993.

Auchincloss, Louis. *Ellen Glasgow.* Minneapolis: U of Minnesota P, 1964.

Backman, Melvin. *Faulkner: The Major Years.* Bloomington: Indiana UP, 1966.

Bailey, Fred Arthur. *Class and Tennessee's Confederate Generation.* Chapel Hill: U of North Carolina P, 1987.

Batteau, Allen W. The *Invention of Appalachia.* Tucson: U of Arizona P, 1990.

Beatty, Richmond, Floyd C. Watkins, Thomas Daniel Young, Randall Steward, eds. *The Literature of the South.* Chicago: Scott, 1952.

Berkowitz, Leonard. "Simple Views of Aggression." *Man and Aggression.* Ed. Ashley Montagu. New York: Oxford UP, 1973. 39-52.

Berry, J. Bill, ed. *Located Lives: Place and Idea in Southern Autobiography.* Athens: U of Georgia P, 1990.

Betten, Neil. "American Attitudes toward the Poor: A Historical Overview." *Current History* 65 (1973): 1-5.

Blair, Walter. *Native American Humor.* New York: American Book, 1937.

Blotner, Joseph. *Faulkner: A Biography.* New York: Random House, 1974.

Boney, F.N. *Southerners All*. Macon: Mercer UP, 1984.

Bradbury, John M. *Renaissance in the South: A Critical History of the Literature, 1920-1960*. Chapel Hill: U of North Carolina P, 1963.

Brooks, Cleanth. "Eudora Welty and the Southern Idiom." *Eudora Welty: Modern Critical Views*. Ed. Harold Bloom. New York: Chelsea House, 1986. 93-107.

———. "The Past Re-examined: *The Optimist's Daughter*." *Mississippi Quarterly* 26 (1973): 577-87.

Bryant, J.A., Jr. *Eudora Welty*. Minneapolis: U of Minnesota P, 1968.

Campbell, Will D. "Used and Abused: The Redneck's Lot." *The Prevailing South: Life and Politics in a Changing Climate*. Ed. Dudley Clendinen. Atlanta: Longstreet P, 1988. 92-104.

Cash, W.J. *The Mind of the South*. New York: Random House-Vintage, 1941.

Collins, Carvel. "Erskine Caldwell at Work." *Conversations with Erskine Caldwell*. Ed. Edwin T. Arnold. Jackson: UP of Mississippi, 1988. 38-51.

Cook, Sylvia Jenkins. *Erskine Caldwell: The Fiction of Poverty, the Flesh and the Spirit*. Baton Rouge: Lousiana State UP, 1991.

Core, George. "Lives Fugitive and Unwritten." Berry 52-65.

Cousins, Paul M. *Joel Chandler Harris: A Biography*. Baton Rouge: Lousiana State UP, 1968.

Dabbs, James McBride. *Who Speaks for the South?* New York: Funk, 1964.

Davenport, Guy. "Appalachian Gothic." *New York Times Book Review* 29 Sept. 1968: 4.

Degler, Carl N. *In Search of Human Nature: The Decline and Revival of Darwinism in American Social Thought*. New York: Oxford UP, 1991.

Eaton, Clement. *The Civilization of the Old South: Writings of Clement Eaton*. Ed. Albert D. Kirwan. Lexington: UP of Kentucky, 1968.

Eckley, Wilton. *Harriette Arnow*. New York: Twayne, 1974.

Elby, Cecil D. "Faulkner and the Southwestern Humorists." *Shenandoah* 11 (Autumn 1959): 13-21.

Flattau, Edward. "Southern Discomfort on Environment." *Arkansas Gazette* 15 July 1990: C3.

Flusche, Michael. "Underlying Despair in the Fiction of Joel Chandler Harris." *Critical Essays on Joel Chandler Harris*. Ed. R. Bruce Bickley, Jr. Boston: Hall, 1981. 174-82.

Flynn, John. "A Journey with Harriette Simpson Arnow." *Michigan Quarterly Review* 29 (1990): 241-60.

Flynt, J. Wayne. *Dixie's Forgotten People: The South's Poor Whites*. Bloomington: Indiana UP, 1979.

Franzen, Jonathan. "Perchance to Dream: In the Age of Images, a Reason to Write Novels." *Harper's* April 1996: 35-54.

Grady, Henry W. *The New South.* New York: Bonner, 1889.

Gretlund, Jan Nordby. "An Interview with Eudora Welty." *Southern Humanities Review* 14 (1980): 193-208.

Grumbach, Doris. "Practitioner of Ghastliness." *New Republic* 9 Feb. 1974: 26-28.

Gwynn, Frederick L., and Joseph L. Blotner. *Faulkner in the University.* Charlottesville: U of Virginia P, 1959.

Hardy, John Edward. "Marrying Down in Eudora Welty's Novels." *Eudora Welty: Critical Essays.* Ed. Peggy Whitman Prenshaw. Jackson: UP of Mississippi, 1979. 93-119.

Harris, Julia Collier, ed. *The Life and Letters of Joel Chandler Harris.* Boston: Houghton, 1918.

Havard, William C., and Walter Sullivan, eds. *A Band of Prophets: The Vanderbilt Agrarians After Fifty Years.* Baton Rouge: Lousiana State UP, 1982.

Hobson, Fred. *The Southern Writer in the Postmodern World.* Athens: U of Georgia P, 1991.

Heyen, William. "A Conversation with James Dickey." *Southern Review* 9 (1973): 135-56.

Hollidy, Carl. *A History of Southern Literature.* 1906. Port Washington: Kennikat, 1969.

Holman, C. Hugh. "The View From the Regency-Hyatt: Southern Social Issues and the Outer World." *Southern Fiction Today.* Ed. George Core. Athens: U of Georgia P, 1969. 16-32.

Hubbell, Jay B. *The South in American Literature 1607-1900.* Durham: Duke UP, 1954.

Hyman, Stanley Edgar. *Flannery O'Connor.* Minneapolis: U of Minnesota P, 1966.

Iggers, Jeremy. "Socially Acceptable Bigotry." *Utne Reader* July-Aug. 1992: 145-46.

Inge, M. Thomas. "Literary Humor of the Old Southwest: A Brief Overview." *Louisiana Studies* 7 (1968): 132-43.

Irelan, Lola M., ed. *Low-Income Life Styles.* Washington, D.C.: U.S. Dept. of Health, Education, and Welfare, 1967.

Jehlen, Myra. *Class and Character in Faulkner's South.* New York: Columbia UP, 1976.

Jones, Jacqueline. *The Dispossessed: America's Underclass from the Civil War to the Present.* New York: Basic Books, 1992.

Jones, John Griffin, ed. *Mississippi Writers Talking.* Jackson: UP of Mississippi, 1982.

Justus, James H. *The Achievement of Robert Penn Warren*. Baton Rouge: Lousiana State UP, 1981.

Kahane, Claire. "The Artificial Nigger." *Massachusetts Review* 19 (1978): 183-98.

Karl, Frederick R. *William Faulkner: American Writer*. New York: Weidenfeld, 1989.

Keen, Sam. *Faces of the Enemy: Reflections of the Hostile Imagination*. San Francisco: Harper, 1986.

Kemble, Francis Anne. *Journal of a Residence on a Georgia Plantation in 1839*. New York: Knopf, 1961.

Korges, James. *Erskine Caldwell*. Minneapolis: U of Minnesota P, 1969.

Landess, Thomas. "The Function of Taste in the Fiction of Eudora Welty." *Mississippi Quarterly* 26 (1973): 543-57.

Lippmann, Walter. *Public Opinion*. New York: Harcourt, 1922.

Lorenz, Konrad. *On Aggression*. Trans. Marjorie Kerr Wilson. New York: Harcourt, 1966.

Lynn, Kenneth S. *Mark Twain and Southwestern Humor*. Westport: Greenwood, 1977.

Lyson, Thomas A. *Two Sides to the Sunbelt: The Growing Divergence Between the Rural and Urban South*. New York: Praeger, 1989.

Magershack, David. *Chekhov: A Life*. New York: Grove, 1952.

Mallard, James. "The Fiction of Social Commitment." *The History of Southern Literature*. Ed. Louis D. Rubin. Baton Rouge: Louisiana State UP, 1985. 351-55.

McDonald, Forrest, and Grady McWhiney. "The South from Self-Sufficiency to Peonage: An Interpretation." *American Historical Review* 85 (1980): 1095-118.

McDonald, W.U., Jr. "Welty's 'Social Consciousness': Revision of 'The Whistle.'" *Modern Fiction Studies* 16 (1970): 193-98.

McDowell, Fredrick P.W. *Elizabeth Madox Roberts*. New York: Twayne, 1963.

McIlwaine, Shields. *The Southern Poor-White from Lubberland to Tobacco Road*. Norman: U of Oklahoma P, 1939.

Millichap, Joseph R. *Robert Penn Warren: A Study of the Short Fiction*. New York, Twayne, 1992.

Montagu, Ashley. *The Nature of Human Aggression*. New York: Oxford UP, 1976.

Morris, Desmond. *The Naked Ape*. New York: McGraw, 1968.

Morris, Michael, and John B. Williamson. "Stereotypes and Social Class: A Focus on Poverty." *In The Eye of the Beholder: Contemporary Issues in Stereotyping*. Ed. Arthur G. Miller. New York: Praeger, 1982. 411-65.

Moss, William M. "Postmodern Georgia Scenes: Harry Crews and the Southern Tradition in Fiction." *A Grit's Triumph: Essays on the Works of Harry Crews.* Ed. David K. Jeffrey. Port Washington: National University Publications, 1983. 33-45.

Newby, I.A. "Getting at the History of Poor Whites in the New South: Some Problems and Possibilities." *Perspectives on the American South: An Annual Review of Society, Politics, and Culture.* Vol. 4. Ed. James C. Cobb and Charles R. Wilson. New York: Gordon and Breach Science Publications, 1987. 81-100.

——. *Plain Folk in the New South: Social Change and Cultural Persistence, 1880-1915.* Lousiana State UP, 1989.

O'Donnell, George Marion. "Faulkner's Mythology." *William Faulkner: Three Decades of Criticism.* Ed. Frederick J. Hoffman and Olga W. Vickery. New York: Harcourt, 1960. 82-93.

Odum, Howard W. *Southern Regions of the United States.* Chapel Hill: U of North Carolina P, 1936.

Page, Walter Hines. *The Rebuilding of Old Commonwealths.* New York: Doubleday, 1902.

Palmer, Tersh. "Interview with Fred Chappell." *Appalachian Journal* 19 (1992): 402-10.

Porter, Katherine Anne. Introduction. *A Curtain of Green and Other Stories.* By Eudora Welty. New York: Harcourt, 1941.

Ridgely J.V. *Nineteenth Century Southern Literature.* Lexington: UP of Kentucky, 1980.

Rossi, Peter H., and Zahava D. Blum. "Class, Status, and Poverty." *On Understanding Poverty.* Ed. Daniel P. Moynihan. New York: Basic Books, 1968. 36-63.

Rubin, Louis D., Jr. *The Faraway Country.* Seattle: U of Washington P, 1963.

——. *A Gallery of Southerners.* Baton Rouge: Lousiana State UP, 1982.

——. *George W. Cable: The Life and Times of a Southern Heretic.* New York: Pegasus, 1969.

Schlesinger, Arthur M., Jr. *The Age of Jackson.* Abridged ed. New York: New American Library, 1962.

Scott, J.P. "The Old-Time Agression." *Man and Aggression.* Ed. Ashley Montagu. New York: Oxford UP, 1973. 136-43.

Shelton, Frank W. "The Poor White Perspective: Harry Crews Among Georgia Writers." *Journal of American Culture* 11.3 (1988): 47-50.

Simkins, Francis Butler. *A History of the South.* New York: Knopf, 1963.

Simpson, Lewis P. "Home by Way of California: The Southerner as the Last European." *Southern Literature and Literary Theory.* Ed. Jefferson Humphries. Athens: U of Georgia P, 1990.

——. "The Southern Discovery of Memory and History." *Sewanee Review* 82 (1974): 1-32.

——. "Southern Fiction." *The Harvard Guide to Contemporary American Writing*. Ed. Daniel Hoffman. Cambridge: Harvard UP, 1979. 153-90.

Skaggs, William H. *The Southern Oligarchy: An Appeal in Behalf of the Silent Masses of Our Country Against the Despotic Rule of the Few*. New York: Devin Adair, 1924.

Somers, Paul, Jr. *Johnson J. Hooper*. Boston: Twayne, 1984.

Stampp, Kenneth M. *The Peculiar Institution*. New York: Vintage, 1956.

Storr, Anthony. *Human Aggression*. New York: Atheneum, 1968.

Sullivan, Walter. "Where Have All the Flowers Gone?" *Sewanee Review* 78 (1970): 654-64.

Tannenbaum, Frank. *Darker Phases of the South*. New York: Putnam, 1924.

Taylor, William R. *Cavalier and Yankee: The Old South and American National Character*. Garden City: Doubleday-Anchor, 1963.

Tindall, George Brown. *The Emergence of the New South: 1913-1945*. Baton Rouge: Louisiana State UP, 1967.

Trent, William P. *William Gilmore Simms*. Boston: Houghton, 1892.

Trilling, Diana. *Claremont Essays*. New York: Harcourt, 1964.

Twelve Southerners. *I'll Take My Stand*. New York: Harper, 1930.

Vande Kieft, Ruth M. *Eudora Welty*. Rev. ed. New Haven: Twayne, 1987.

Walsh, William T. *Speak So I Shall Know Thee: Interviews with Southern Writers*. Jefferson: McFarland, 1990.

Weaver, Richard M. *The Southern Tradition at Bay: A History of Post-Bellum Thought*. Ed. George Core and M.E. Bradford. New Rochelle: Arlington House, 1968.

Weber, Brom. "A Note on Edmund Wilson and George Washington Harris." *The Lovingood Papers*. Ed. Ben Harris McClary. Athens: The Sut Society, 1962.

West, Paul. *Robert Penn Warren*. Minneapolis: U of Minnesota P, 1964.

Westling, Louise. *Eudora Welty*. London: Macmillan, 1989.

Wiggonton, Eliot. "The Mountains: A Different Mix of Politics." *The Prevailing South*. Ed. Dudley Clendinen. Atlanta: Longstreet P, 1988. 150-67.

Wiley, Bell Irvin. The *Plain People of the Confederacy*. Chicago: Quadrangle Books, 1963.

Wilhelm, Albert E. "An Interview with Bobbie Ann Mason." *Southern Quarterly* 26.2 (1988): 27-38.

Williams, Cratis D. "The Southern Mountaineer in Fact and Fiction." *Appalachian Journal* 3 (1976): 334-92.

Wilson, Edmund. *Patriotic Gore: Studies in the Literature of the American Civil War.* New York: Oxford UP, 1962.

Woodward, C. Vann. *Origins of the New South, 1877-1913.* Baton Rouge: Louisiana State UP, 1951.

——. "The Search for Southern Identity." *Myth and Southern History: The New South.* Vol. 2. Ed. Patrick Gerster and Nicholas Cords. Urbana: U of Illinois P, 1989. 119-32.

Young, Thomas Daniel. *The Past in the Present: A Thematic Study of Modern Southern Fiction.* Baton Rouge: Louisiana State UP, 1981.

# Index